Memories
of
Glasgow

Part of the
Memories
series

*The Publishers would like to thank the following companies for supporting
the production of this book*

The Annan Gallery (T & R Annan & Sons Limited)

British Aerospace Royal Ordnance

Cardowan Creameries Limited

The Crolla Ice Cream Company Limited

J&J Denholm Limited

D McGhee & Sons Limited

Glasgow College of Nautical Studies

JH Lightbody & Son Limited

McKean & Company Limited

Andrew Muirhead & Son Limited

Ross & Liddell Limited

Southern Coaches (NM) Limited

Stow College

Thomas Tunnock Limited

First published in Great Britain by True North Books Limited
Units 3 - 5 Heathfield Industrial Park
Elland West Yorkshire
HX5 9AE
Tel. 01422 377977
© Copyright: True North Books Limited 1999

ISBN 1 900463 68 7

Text, design and origination by True North Books Limited, Elland, West Yorkshire
Printed and bound by The Amadeus Press Limited, Huddersfield, West Yorkshire

Memories are made of this

Memories. We all have them; some good, some bad, but our memories of the city we grew up in are usually tucked away in a very special place in our minds. The best are usually connected with our childhood and youth, when we longed to be grown up and paid no attention to adults who told us to enjoy being young, as these were the best years of our lives. We look back now and realise that they were right.

So many memories - perhaps of the war and rationing, perhaps of parades, celebrations and Royal visits. And so many changes; one-way traffic systems and pedestrianisation. New trends in shopping led that to the very first self-serve stores being opened.

Through the bad times and the good, however, Glasgow not only survived but prospered. We have only to look at the city as it is today, with its finest buildings now cleaned and restored to their full glory, and the traditional tourist attractions now complemented by up-to-the-minute facilities, to see what progress has been realised and what achievements have been made over the last 50 years. Glasgow has a history to be proud of - but more importantly, a great future to look forward to, into the new millennium and beyond.

Contents

The streets of change

Seen on Trongate, this chap was looking dapper in the large flat cap that was part of the uniform of the working man. He might be exchanging it for a tin helmet soon. The year is 1914 and events in Serbia are to lead the world into a war the like of which it had never before seen. Instead of the stroll from Glasgow Cross, our subject could be ploughing through the mud and horror of Passchendale and the Somme, his mates falling in a hail of bullets. To the right is the old Tron church. Drunken vandals burned it down in 1793. The steeple survived and a new church built behind it. It is now the Tron Theatre. Trongate was one of four main medieval streets. It was once called St Thenew's Gait, which was corrupted into St Enoch's Gate. The name came from a chapel at its west end, dedicated to the mother of St Kentigern. It used to run as far as the city's west port, where there was a twin spouted well. The name Trongate came into being in the 16th century. The city had gained the right to keep a free tron or weigh bar that was located here. The importance of the district receded as the city centre moved from the Cross. Buchanan Street and Sauchiehall Street became the focus of a classier sort of customer and around Trongate slipped into a time of decay, only improved by the slum clearance of the Victorian age. Further east, beyond the Cross, was some of Glasgow's worst housing. If the man we are looking at was from that end of the city, perhaps he was happy to escape for a quiet hour or two.

Above: Tramcars, loaded with travellers on their way to who knows what or where, clank across Jamaica Bridge. They seem to be led by a limousine in some sort of convoy or parade. On top you felt rather superior as you watched the world scurry by beneath your feet. It was a time of change, one of many in the 20th century. The Great War had been fought and the free world was rebuilding, at a cost. Andrew Bonar Law, a partner in one of the city's largest iron manufacturing and exporting firms, had briefly been Prime Minister. But, by the following year, 1924, Britain would see its first Labour government. The majority of the tram-riders would have been happy with that. Towering above the cars, carts and pedestrians, those on the upper decks had a fine view up and down the river. If they could look out 70 years later, there would be some 14 bridges to take in. There are now seven traffic, four pedestrian, two railway and one motorway bridge to contend with. Towards the end of the 18th century there was but one medieval bridge for all cross-river transport. It had been built in 1450. The one in the picture was the third on this site and is also known as Glasgow Bridge. On wintry days, Glaswegians would have been grateful for a warming cup of Bovril, advertised in the lower left of the picture. A steaming cup of the tangy beef extract warmed the cockles of many a chilled heart and their fingers and throats, too!

Right: This elevated view shows a number of the varied features that mark out Glasgow as a special city. The marvellous architecture in the foreground is repeated throughout its many elegant streets. There are beautifully preserved Victorian buildings, none more splendid than the City Chambers. In and around there are unique examples of the renowned designer, Charles Rennie Mackintosh. The famous Glasgow School of Art is another of his masterpieces. Alexander Thomson, known for his Greek style, has also contributed to the interesting Glasgow skyline. Balanced against those delights are the memories of the worst of the architecture, as can be seen to the left. Long rows of tenement buildings stood as a depressing testament to the poverty and deprivation which affected so many Glaswegians in the late 19th and early 20th centuries. They stood like ugly giants above the shoppers and passers-by on the streets below. The centre of the photograph is a reminder of the reliance we had upon the tram as the main means of transport in the city. Long avenues of cobbled roads were cut down the middle by the lines of the tracks. The tramcars followed one another in a constant procession up and down the streets, so popular and necessary were they for us to carry out our everyday life. That is until September 1962 when the last of the trams took its final run into the history books.

Bottom: The electric trams, seen here at the Jamaica Street/Argyle Street junction, used to run three abreast along here. After the Great War, the increase in car ownership meant that some part of the carriageway had to be given over to the motor-car. Trams still dominated the streets, as can be seen from this 1930 photograph. It looks to be a busy day for shoppers and hundreds upon hundreds will have travelled in by public transport. The days of the out of town shopping centre or the pedestrianised ways and arcades are still half a century away. One way systems and multi-storey car parks belong to a time not yet envisaged by the shoppers seen here. Argyle Street, which is really a continuation of Trongate, was originally Westergait and then Anderston Walk. It became Argyll (later Argyle) Street in 1751. The name was to mark the connection with the 1st Duke of Argyll. His title had been created in 1701 as a reward for political services. Further back, the origins of Argyle Street are hidden. The section running east from Buchanan Street, towards the Cross, has a flavour of an older and less cosmopolitan Glasgow. It is only in later times that the east enders went any further west to do their shopping. It is Argyle Street that exiles from the city remember as the centre of commerce and trade of their city roots. You can find an occasional Argyle Street in far off parts of the Commonwealth. Is this a case of MacKilroy was here?

Right: Looking at the George V Bridge in 1929, it must have been a quiet part of the day. Normally, there would have been a fairly heavy throng of people and traffic shuffling along. Perhaps we're looking at the Glasgow equivalent of siesta time. However, there may be another reason. It is the era of the depression. After the so-called war to end all wars, the poverty and unemployment of the late 20s gave little reason for many to be out and about. Black Thursday, the day of the American Wall Street crash, was upon us, and a second Labour government was to coming to office. Then, people turned away from the Tories and Liberals in times of unrest with the hope that the new social policies would help put bread on the table. Fat chance, some might have said. The bridge in view has some similarities with its neighbour, Jamaica (Glasgow) Bridge, which is to the right of the railway bridge you can see. The parapet of the George V Bridge could almost be a carbon copy. However, there are only three arches. In fact, these are not true arches, being disguised spans of concrete box girders. Reinforced with concrete, the roadway is 80 ft wide and runs 412 ft from Commerce Street to Oswald Street. It was opened in 1928. In the previous century, this stretch of the Clyde used to see small steamers travel to such far-flung destinations as Stornoway and London, Sligo and Southampton.

Off on its way to Kelvinside, passing the cake and grocery store, the tram is taking shoppers and office workers to their homes in the northwest end of Glasgow. It will go out past the Victorian splendour of Kelvingrove Park and the less than splendid tenements on the way. However, these were less depressing than those on the other side of the city. There were also some grand houses around there, which have since become offices. St Vincent Street, coming away from Blythswood Hill, is home to the Strathclyde Regional Council Offices, with the large Abbey National Building Society structure on the opposite side. The grey marble and the glass of the Whyte and Mackay office contrasts with the appearance of the Gaelic Church of Scotland and the Free Church of Scotland which cling to the past. The oddly named Drum and Monkey bar doesn't quite have the same ring of importance. Above it all, towers the Hilton building, which casts its shadow from nearby Bothwell Street Offices have been a feature of St Vincent Street throughout the 20th century. One of the most impressive dates back to 1924. This is the Bank of Scotland's main Glasgow office. As it cuts across Renfield Street, the grandeur of its pillars are quite breathtaking. Designed by James Miller, it drew heavily on the architecture of a bank that lay on Broadway in New York.

Right: The formation of Jamaica Street in 1751 gave the western end of Argyle Street an opening southwards to the second bridge over the Clyde. Seen in 1905, at the junction of the two streets, the elegant dress of the time is to be seen in the lady, as she certainly was, centre picture. Perhaps she was on her way to Kate Cranston's Willow Tea Rooms or for high tea at the Kenilworth Hotel, before a visit to the theatre and a soirée with a gentleman friend. He was sure to have the long side-whiskers and twirling moustache of the day. The full-length dress and the gathered fabric of the bustle, underneath the trimmed hat, mark her as a woman of distinction. Certainly, her clothing would have been readily available locally. Because of the availability of materials from other engineering works, the American Singer Sewing Machine Co set up in business in the 1860s. By the 1880s there were 25 other such factories. Cotton and the textile industry were important to the city. However, competition from the North of England had eroded Glasgow's importance in this field by the end of the 19th century. The name of Jamaica Street is a good reminder of another source of some of the city's early prosperity. In the 1700s, men, known as the 'tobacco lords', made their fortunes by investing in trade in tobacco with the American colonies. Profits were invested in West Indian sugar and in cotton growing.

Below: Cowlairs Co-operative Society dominated the retail outlets at Springburn Cross. As well as the shops carrying its own name, most of the other businesses operated from premises owned by the Co-op. From their rents Cowlairs Co-op got its own form of 'divi' which helped the payouts made to its customer members. Ticking little stamps on cards was part of the shopping experience. When the card was full it could be exchanged, for goods bought at the Co-op, of course. It is an unusually quiet scene because the Cross was the centre of a lively community. By 1900 the population here had grown to 30,000. This was a vibrant working class district. Most were in employment connected with the railway. The majority lived in the tenements that had become part and parcel of Glasgow life. Rents were often paid annually. This presented budgeting problems for the less sophisticated worker. Saving for future commitments at the Clydesdale and North of Scotland bank at the corner of Cowlairs Rd did not come easily. People were happier to live for today and to pay as they went. Needless to say, some fell into debt and were preyed upon by moneylenders charging exorbitant rates. In 1912 a law was passed forcing landlords to lease properties for shorter periods. Council house building did not take off until 1924, when the first Labour government came to power.

Above: Over a century ago, the horse-drawn trams trundled across the Jamaica Street Bridge. It was still a time when horsepower meant just what it said. In 1894, Rudyard Kipling was putting the finishing touches to the Jungle Book and Queen Victoria reigned on, seemingly forever. Newish companies were springing up, such as Nestlé, the Swiss manufacturer. Now a household name, back then it was less than 30 years old. It had been founded on the business of providing baby milk products. The street hoarding was a principal form of advertising in those days before the cinema, radio or television. Not many working folk bothered with newspapers and the billboard, placed on a busy thoroughfare, was certain to grab the attention of the Victorian passerby. This bridge was one of Glasgow's main places to cross the Clyde. It was the second such bridge on this site. By its very name, the link with the colonies was retained. Exports of cotton goods to Jamaica had been worth as much as £646,227 in the year of 1810, when the trade was in its heyday. At this time, 10 per cent of the ship tonnage passing through the port was connected with the Caribbean island. This particular bridge, opened in 1866 after some 33 years of preparatory work from the date of the laying of the foundation stone, had not long to run. Its replacement was only five years away. The horses would soon clip-clop into history, as well. The artificial power of electricity and the internal combustion engine weren't too far off in replacing those noble beasts.

Top: Away to the right, Springburn Rd, Flemington Rd and Atlas Rd sweep away towards the rail stations at Springburn and Barnhill. Opposite, Keppochill Rd runs away towards the recreation ground at Cowlairs Park. In the 1950s local residents happily went about their business and went off to work at the workshops and repair yards at Cowlairs and St Rollox. Others were involved in the locomotive building taking place at the Hydepark and Atlas works. The North British Locomotive Company was the largest of its kind in Europe. Beeching changed that. His report of 1965 led to the scaling down of the national industry by closing many branch lines and stations. Our failure to adapt from steam to diesel-electric saw the closure of the NBL and the Cowlairs workshop. The community was suddenly thrown into an era of massive unemployment. Allied with the run down of the housing, large numbers of people were rehoused in estates at Castlemilk, Easterhoue and Cumbernauld. Springburn was demolished in the name of urban redevelopment. No longer could you go to McNee's for some bath salts for mum's birthday present or to the dentist's on the first floor at Keppochill Rd corner. That last visit was one well worth forgetting. The needle and the old, slow drill hurt. That was one part of the nostalgic trip that hasn't become a rosy memory with the passing of the years.

The grandly carved buildings on Renfield Street, leading north from the city centre, stand majestically above the line of trams on their way to Mosspark and Pollokshields. These areas are now cut by the M77, one of the motorway links criss-crossing the city borders. Back in 1936, public transport carried the people of Glasgow to and from the city to carry out their business or to do their shopping. It is only from such an elevated view that the magnificence of the architecture can be appreciated. Down below, the people, scurrying like little ants, would get an awful crick in the neck trying to look up to the top of the buildings which made their

birth place such a thing of beauty. For some, living conditions inside their own homes left a lot to be desired, but the work of the old planners and builders could only be admired. Sensibly, the majority of the shoppers have copied the words of the popular song and crossed to the sunny side of the street. On a day like this, it is unlikely that Reid & Co (lower right) would have sold many of their brollies. As trunk makers of distinction, they might have made the odd sale to someone packing up his winter clothes for storage until the chilly weather returned. But, today the sun was shining on the righteous, and everyone else, on Renfield Street.

Below: Much criticised by purists for scarring the city, though it is hard to see how we can move without it, the M8 motorway has ripped through what was the St George's Cross of 1938. All sorts of shops could be found around here in those last days of uneasy peace before the second world war. The House of Fraser, which once dominated Glasgow's shopping scene with a large number of outlets, owned the Wood and Selby store. Other competing shops and stores included Duncan's and Woolworth's, both of which were on the right hand side, looking east. Duncan's sold fine hosiery and gloves. No proper lady of the late 30s would be seen around town without her gloves. To be so improperly dressed was regarded as 'common'. The store, known to everyone throughout most of the 20th century as 'Woolies', was the original 'five and ten cent store'. The girls on the till never seemed to know the price of anything and 'How much is it, love?' seemed to be part of the vocabulary they had been taught in training. Most of the housing here was in four

storey tenement blocks. These overcrowded and insanitary buildings were nearly all knocked down in the redevelopment push of the late 60s. St George's Cross was a very busy junction, feeding traffic from Springburn, Maryhill and Possilpark into the city centre. The traffic policeman at the crossroads is in for an active day.

Bottom: The coming of the M8 motorway has changed the nature of this most famous of streets forever. Ask anyone from outside the city to name a place in Glasgow and 'Sauchiehall Street' is sure to be the answer. The name is supposed to have come from the willow trees that grew on the wetland 'haughs', so a form of 'soggy haugh' might have been the origin of the place name. Whatever the truth of it, Sauchiehall Street was the main shopping centre and source of entertainment. The tramtracks ran along its full length, all the way to Kelvingrove, carrying cars of shoppers and visitors to its cinemas, clubs, department stores and galleries. When the trams disappeared in the early 60s, the eastern end was pedestrianised. However, the precinct in this area wouldn't be officially opened until 1988. The large stores closed and by the 70s it had lost its rank as the number one street in the city. When the motorway cut across it at Charing Cross, much of the western end turned its lovely mansions into offices of one sort or another. In 1928, the street was in its prime. On the right is the Picture House, which had opened in 1910. It later became the Gaumont and continued until 1972, being replaced by the Savoy Market. The photo shows a time when the film world was changing forever. Hollywood had just introduced the 'talkie'. Now we could hear as well as see our favourites, like the world's sweetheart, Mary Pickford. Who at the Picture House didn't also swoon at the good looks of her husband, Douglas Fairbanks, in such swashbucklers as the 'Iron Mask'.

Above: Between the two world wars Glasgow struggled to compete with the emerging overseas markets. Unemployment was high. Although the great shipyards of the Clyde were still able to build the big liners, these sorts of contracts were few and far between. Other industries were in similar decline. At the beginning of the 20th century Glasgow was the 'second city of the Empire'. As one of the finest and richest cities in Europe its museums, galleries and public buildings were the envy of all. The retail outlets and businesses along Renfield Street mirrored the success of the other important streets in the area. Busy bowler-hatted men, on their way to the office, used to vie with the barrow boys selling secondhand books. The Council would later ban these booksellers as they were thought to lower the tone of the district. But, as the purse strings were tightened, establishments like RG Lawrie found life becoming tougher. Flags were flying bravely above the doorway as if to show a pride in still being there. Across the passage there is a hint of trouble times ahead. 'Great offers' are being advertised. Flourishing businesses didn't make reductions. Those fighting to survive had to. Renfield Street, in this era, was also a place of rest and recreation. The Regent and Green's Playhouse cinemas attracted those seeking escapism and the many tea rooms those in need of a quiet break from the strains of everyday life.

The long avenue of Sauchiehall Street stretches east from Charing Cross. The Coronation trams, a permanent feature on Glasgow's streets in 1938, were a new line, having replaced the older and less reliable Standards. Making their way towards the Grand Hotel, from where this photograph was taken, passengers might have been getting off at the corner on the right. If so, it could have been to pay a visit to William Skinner's Tea Rooms. Skinner's was just one of a number of such fashionable places to take light refreshment in the middle of a shopping spree. Cranston's and Craig's were rivals who also offered a good standard of service. Situated on the corner of Newton Street, which is now flanked by the motorway, Skinner opened his business here in 1835. It would continue as a going concern until tastes changed and the demand for the relaxed atmosphere of the tea room was no longer needed. It closed in 1961. Opposite, McColl's shop had a clock face set into the building. The face later vanished, but became a working clock once more in 1970. Glasgow, in 1999 the UK city of architecture and design, has held a number of important exhibitions over the years. The Grand Hotel had seen many famous visitors to its steps and, in 1938, played host to visitors to the Empire Exhibition, centred at Bellahouston Park. Fifty years before this photo, the Prince of Wales (later to be Edward VII) had left to open the International Exhibition at Kelvingrove.

Above: Before the days of the National Lottery the football pools gave punters the best hope of scooping a large cash prize. Vernon's was one of two major companies offering hope. Forty years ago a six figure prize was wealth beyond the wildest dreams of the man in the street. Come to think about it, it's not to be sniffed at come the start of a new millennium. As this pipe dream on the tram passes along Trongate and away from the steeple, further along on the left, towards Argyle Street, note the clothiers. In grandma's time there was a host of such shops around here. From late Victorian times, with the coming of the sewing machine, the making of clothes became a factory based industry because of the speed of these machines and the volume that could be handled. The factories sold direct to shops, as well as exporting their goods. D & H Cohen made all the skirts and trousers sold by the huge chain of Marks and Spencer. They also specialised in uniforms for schoolchildren. You didn't go to be educated in a T shirt and denims as happens now. Short grey trousers and a regulation shirt and tie were expected. Watch out the girl who appeared with a tunic hem that did not touch the ground when she knelt down. The school blazer was the ultimate in unisex clothing, as long as you didn't notice which way the buttons ran.

Above right: The Scottish Daily Mail has the news that really counts, according to the advert on the tram. But what was the news these women were discussing? By the look of the buttonhole of the man on the right, there may well have been a wedding taking place nearby. If so, the talk would centre on the bride and how pretty she looked. The poor old bridegroom hardly favoured a mention, unless he was hungover from the stag night.

Then his sickly pallor would have earned a reproachful look or two. He was there to make up the numbers and because he had to be. He was someone's proud son, but today wasn't his day. That belonged to his future wife and her mother. For weeks beforehand, the wedding outfit and going away suit would have been at the centre of everything. On this special day, that visit to the hairdresser was the finishing touch to all the hours of tension that would only be relieved by mum's tears when she told everybody how happy she was. Whilst the women nattered on, the men patiently waited at the roadside. There would soon be a pint or two to make all this hanging about worthwhile. In the meantime, the hat and headscarf brigade continued to hold court. The scene was culled from a time of the middle of the 20th century, but it was one that had been seen on countless days before and would be again in the future.

Below: The clock tower of the Tron dates back to around 1593, when the first Queen Elizabeth was on the throne. The steeple came along some 40 years later, when Charles I, grandson of Mary, Queen of Scots, was the British monarch. The home of the public weigh beam is now all that is left of the original Tron church that had been begun in 1484. It was then called the Collegiate Church of St Mary and St Anne. Destroyed in a fire in 1793, it was rebuilt to the south and independent of the steeple. The designer, John Carrick, inserted arches into it in 1855. This was done to allow pedestrian access. Over the road from the Scottish Clothing Company, the dress and hair style of the pedestrians is typical of the early 1960s period. Men still went out onto the streets in their suits and collars and ties. Their hair was cut conservatively, with just a hint of a quif, if you were a little bit trendy or adventurous. The women's hair was uniformly on the short side, with an element of the permanent wave to keep it in shape. The one fashion item missing was the hat. Almost overnight the need to have headcover disappeared. For men, the caps and hats were a statement of social class. For women, headwear was only proper if you were to be thought of as a lady. Not any more, and milliners everywhere cursed their luck.

Bottom: It's a quieter day at Charing Cross. Sauchiehall Street reaches down towards its junction with Renfield Street in the far distance. Money is tight. The shops don't have the same amount or variety of goods to sell as before the war. Rationing is biting. In 1949, the ration coupon had been with us since the start of the decade. It wouldn't finally become a thing of the past until 1955. Transport changes were coming subtly to the city's streets by now. The tram, although it would still be around for another ten or a dozen years, was losing its influence as the main form of public transport. More double decker buses were on the road and this was the year that saw the introduction of the trolley bus. A strange cross between the bus and the tram, with its pantograph reaching up to grab electricity from the overhead cables, the trolley lasted less than 20 years before it left our streets. Somehow, the trolley bus seemed more like a giant dodgem. Not many bemoaned their passing. The same couldn't be said of the loss of the 'caurs' when that came. Charing Cross marked the end of the entertainment and shopping focus which was Sauchiehall Street. This is even more marked today because the M8 provides a physical barrier to the west end of the city. Charing Cross Mansions is one of the few buildings here to have survived the regeneration and development of the 70s.

Above: It was a good pull up the hill coming away from Balgrayhill. The cyclist would have been glad to get on a flatter stretch and draw breath. Even Reg Harris, the British cycling champion of the 1950s, would have found it a tough haul. These pictures are the only real way to hold on to memories of old Springburn. The name probably comes from the various springs and burns which used to be seen in the 18th century countryside here. These were buried under the old railway lines and housing of the Victorian age. But the well kept landmarks of the 20th century have gone as well. Nearby was the Springburn North UF church at the corner with Elmvale Street. United in 1967 with Springburn Hill, the vacant church was vandalised and then demolished. Above Maguire's pub were the Argyll Halls that held dances and various other social functions. The pub became Healy's Terminus bar and the Halls a singing lounge. Ex Celtic footballer, Chris Shelvane, later owned it. These days and those that went before can only be recalled properly by artefacts and photographs. As fewer of those who lived through the time remain with the passage of time, community museums, like the one at Atlas Square become more important. Only by preserving these can future generations gain an accurate picture of the past.

Right: A sunny late summer day in the 1950s, with the lengthening shadows falling across Springburn Rd. Beyond the Kirkcaldy Linoleum Market, the low building on the right is the railway station. The Cowlairs Co-operative Society on the left was just one of 110 outlets across the city. Based in this fiercely working class district, which saw families supporting one other, the Co-op provided competitors with problems. The dividend it paid was one of the highest of its type. As other shops also found that their landlord was also the Co-op, they could be forgiven for thinking that they were on a hiding to nothing in trying to compete. These were the streets that were the playground for the comedy actress, Molly Weir. Her fame spread from local reps and concert parties down to the theatres and studios of London. Springburn was proud to see one of its daughters return via the TV screen in a number of character parts in plays and sitcoms. She wouldn't have recognised it these days. The Royal cinema has gone. Formerly the Ideal, it had started life as Springburn Electric Theatre. Gone, too, is the fire station, which was near the corner with Keppochill Rd. In 1986 that part was converted into flats and modern housing for elderly residents. The fire station had dealt with a huge fire at the Oxford Picture House in 1941. When it moved to Petershill Rd, guess what was next door - a cinema!

Bottom: The Morris Minor leads the little convoy up Springburn Rd at the junction with Cowlairs Rd to the right. The old Cowlairs Works had built tanks for the battlefields of World War I. The centre of the locomotive industry was based there from the 1860s onwards. The Hydepark Works was the largest of its type in Europe, exporting to places worldwide. Glasgow's first railway line, to Garnkirk, opened in 1831 and its bridge crossed Springburn Rd nearer the city centre. As we look on this scene from the 1950s, it's poignant to see the bus following the tram. Before too long, it would overtake the tram in importance and the latter would be dead and buried within a few short years. Brooke Bond Tea, being advertised on the side of the bus, has given us some of the more memorable of TV adverts. Who can't help but smile at the antics of the chimps supping their tea and displaying human tendencies? With the clever scripts and voice-overs, they have become some of the best-loved characters to have come onto our screens. It must be because we can remember those days of the chimps' tea parties that were put on at the zoo for our enjoyment. Nostalgia is a powerful tool. The Midland Bank on the corner is now nationally a part of the Hong Kong and Shanghai Banking Corporation. It doesn't quite sound the same, somehow.

Right: Pictured on Argyle Street, not far from the Tron on Trongate, this old chap has seen better days. Who knows what difficulties have brought him to spend his life in a state of hopeless despair. He might have been a hero of the second world war of 20 years before, when he fought to enable the young schoolboy coming towards him to be free. Maybe it's his own fault that he's fallen on hard times, the Schweppes in the window or the Irn Bru across the road not being his favourite tipple. Certainly, the demon drink has caused the break up of family life and the fall of many to become down and outs. But, we mustn't judge. The demise of the heavy industry of the shipyards and the railways saw thousands of jobs disappear. Men who had brought home bulging pay packets were, along with the ships they built, on the scrapheap. Being unable to provide for the family any more drove so many over the edge. As the pedestrians move towards him, will any give him a second glance, or will heads be discreetly turned away? If we don't see the problem, then it doesn't exist. Not for us, at any rate, but he is left to tramp the pavements looking for a few bob for a meal and a place to rest his head for the night. Folk singer Ralph McTell used to ask, 'Have you seen the old man who walks the streets of London?' Maybe not, but we've seen more than enough on the streets of Glasgow.

In sickness and in health

Above: The beginning of Glasgow's campaign to eradicate the scourge of tuberculosis from the city was marked by an official launch in George Square. It was March 9th, 1957, and the gathering of 10,000 people on that Saturday evening was entertained by the band of the Highland Light Infantry and the Glasgow Police Pipe Band as they waited for the speeches and the cutting of a ribbon outside the X-Ray Centre by two youngsters which would signal the start of Europe's biggest ever health improvement campaign. Specially-positioned searchlights painted patterns in the sky and a fireworks display would later enthrall the crowds as 37 athletes carried Olympic-style torches with the 'X-ray' message to every Ward in the city.

Among the runners taking part were famous names such Dunky Wright and marathon men Ian Binnie and Graham Everett. The speech-making began at 7.30 p.m, with the Lord Provost, Mr Andrew Hood, The Secretary of State for Scotland, Mr J.S Maclay, and Mr John Mains, Convenor of the Health and Welfare Committee of Glasgow emphasising the need for everyone over the age of 14 years to be X-rayed during the coming five weeks. The incidence of TB in Glasgow was higher than anywhere else in Europe - and almost three times higher than the rest of Britain. Every day an average of 17 new cases were diagnosed on average in the city. A target of 250,000 X-ray examinations was set for the campaign.

Bottom: A floodlit George Square was the venue for the launch of the Glasgow campaign against tuberculosis in 1957. The campaign would last five weeks and break all records as the largest of its type ever to be seen in Europe. TB had long been a problem in Glasgow where the highest incidence of the disease existed of anywhere in Europe. Over 6000 new cases had been reported in 1956, slightly down on the previous year, but still a huge burden on local medical resources and the local community. It was estimated that the disease cost the city over £1 million each year - on top of the inestimable cost in terms of human misery. New drugs and treatments meant that it was worthwhile to identify people with the disease so that they could be treated and the spread of infection curtailed. Everyone over the age of 14 should be screened by X-ray, a process which would take less than a minute - with 'no undressing required'. A similar, but far smaller campaign had been waged against diphtheria in the area. That disease had caused 226 deaths in 1940 from 5000 recorded cases. By 1955 and 1956 no deaths were attributed to the disease and only a handful of cases were recorded. The same success rate was hoped for with the campaign against tuberculosis.

Right: An impressive convoy of mobile X-ray stations was gathered from all over Britain prior to the start of Glasgow's five-week TB campaign in 1957. Four of the vehicles had been lent by the Army and a further 21 from the English National Health Service. Shortly before this scene was

recorded on the outskirts of the city the convoy had grouped together on the Penrith North road. It was the largest peace-time health convoy ever known. The whole campaign had been organised like a major military operation - indeed, it had to be, if the crippling disease was to be tackled effectively. The slogan adopted for the campaign was "Earlier discovery - quicker recovery". These mobile units would be positioned around Glasgow so that there would be no excuse for anyone not turning up for their X-ray. Each mobile X-ray station was supported by at least one double decker bus equipped with extra lights and heating to create a mobile waiting room. New drugs and new treatment would ensure that cases which were detected could be treated more effectively. Additional hospital beds, doctors and nurses were in place to treat these cases, expected to number about three in every 1000 people tested.

Sunday March 10th, the day after the launch of the campaign, saw an impressive parade of mobile X-ray units in the city centre. The Lord Provost 'took the salute' as the heavy trucks, laden with state of the art equipment, snaked their way around the narrow streets, much to the delight of the cheering crowds. In all, 30 mobile X-ray units had been draughted in for the campaign; 24 from England, and six from other areas of Scotland. Each vehicle weighed 10 tons and was 26ft in length. The trucks were manned by one doctor, two nurses, four clerks, two typists and the driver. The mobile units were located on 16 permanent sites and, in addition, some of the larger factories were visited for the added convenience of their staff.

Left: Every available means of publicity was employed in order to promote awareness of the TB campaign. This illuminated tram carried the message around the city, proclaiming "Everybody over 14 years X-Ray now" and reassuring people of the ease, confidentiality and need *not* to undress for the X-ray. The message was put across at football clubs, cinemas and other places of entertainment. A light aircraft from Nottingham was enlisted to fly over the city with a recorded message urging people to have the test blaring out from powerful loudspeakers. Crawling across the skies at a height of 1500ft the speakers proclaimed 'Go to the nearest X-ray centre and get your friends too go as well!' Nothing was left to chance in the drive to make sure that everyone knew about the campaign, and that massive resources were all in place to treat the new cases which were predicted to come to light. In the end around 7000 new cases were found, and the second phase of the campaign, effecting treatment, was soon underway.

Below: Queues at the main X-ray centres in George Square were extensive - even when the weather was less than pleasant. The X-ray itself was said to take only a fraction of a second once the 'patient' had managed to secure his or her place in the booth. Official 'hostesses' would look after any accompanying children while mum or dad had their X-ray. There were two queues - one for men and the other for women at each centre. Up to 300 people per hour passed through the main units in the centre of Glasgow, and additional city centre screening facilities were provided at two large department stores. There were many unsung heroes associated with this, the biggest ever health improvement campaign, not least of which being the army of clerical staff and typists tasked with ensuring that everyone tested received their results within four days of their visit. The first day of the campaign saw over 20,000 people tested - a world record in itself. By the third day over 80,000 people had had their test, and confidence was high that the 250,000 target for the campaign would soon be smashed.

Scotland's own Jimmy Logan was one of the first to sign up as a volunteer helper in the TB campaign. He was not alone, for the massive undertaking relied upon the help of no less than 11,000 volunteers who had freely given their time to play a part in the fight against TB. An obvious use of Jimmy's talents was to promote the awareness of the campaign. He was soon asked to record a song with that aim, called "An X-Ray For Me". The song was sung to the tune of "A Gordon For Me" with words written by Archie Gentles, a member of staff at Glasgow Corporation Health and Welfare Department. Musical accompaniment was supplied by a combination of the Glasgow Alhambra Orchestra and the Scottish National Orchestra. Dr. William Horne, the Chief Medical Officer praised Jimmy Logan's contribution to the campaign, saying that every possible publicity method must be used because the task was so important that nothing must be left to chance.

and football grounds. Other methods employed to encourage the young to come forward for their X-rays included the staging of a film premier, *The Rainmaker* at the Gaumont, and the deployment of a light aircraft broadcasting a loudspeaker message over the streets of the city and public events such as football matches. Greta Reid, vocalist, can be seen here with Bill Lambert's band - Bill himself is pictured with his treasured saxophone.

Top: Looking back, you have to hand it to the organisers of the TB campaign for the thoroughness of the operation. Not only did they pull together all the resources necessary to test a phenomenal number of people, but they also created massive amounts of publicity and awareness for the campaign to ensure that local people

Above: Glasgow's anti-TB campaign would only be a success if it persuaded all age groups (over 14 years) to take part. From the start it was recognised that younger people may be difficult to influence, and at least two songs were written and performed to help get the message across. This picture shows Bill Lambert and his band performing the song "X-Ray Rock". The song was written by a local health worker, Doctor Bill Thomson, with music by his friend Alex Bunting, a chartered surveyor in the city. After a recording of the tune by Bill Lambert and his band was approved by the Medical Officer of Health the order was given to produce 'dozens' of records to be played at dance halls, cinemas

would actually *turn up* and be tested. One tool in their armoury was a promotion designed to give everyone having an X-ray the chance to win exciting prizes. These ranged from a family saloon car (an Austin A35, complete with insurance and concrete garage!) to a washing machine, television set, holiday in the Highlands and a bedroom suite. all the prizes were sponsored by local firms. In this picture Max Bygraves (who was appearing at the Glasgow Empire) can be seen presenting the prize of a washing machine to David Henderson (second from the right), a 35 year old polisher from Drumchapel. Max Bygraves had his own X-ray after the presentation was completed.

GLASGOW X-RAY CAMPAIGN

11th MARCH — 12th APRIL 1957

The **SCOTTISH GAS BOARD**

DONATED THIS GAS REFRIGERATOR AS A PRIZE TO BE AWARDED DURING THE GLASGOW X-RAY CAMPAIGN.

YOUR NAME WILL BE INCLUDED IN THE DRAW IF YOU UNDERGO AN.....

X-RAY

the NEW Electrolux *silent refrigerator*

Such was the attraction of the prize draw in the TB campaign, that several reports of people having two or more X-rays were reported, these people being referred to as 'twicers' - their actions intended to give them an extra chance of winning one of the exciting prizes on offer. The famous American pop singer Johnnie Ray in the 1950s and he is seen here presenting a fridge to 14 year-old Sandra Stevenson of Maryhill. At £70 this would have been a luxurious item in 1957 for sure. Reports from the time describe how Sandra was called from her maths class to the headmasters' office to be told of her win. Her main concern was her meeting with her pop idol. "I am awfully thrilled to be meeting

Johnnie Ray - I wish I knew what to say to him!" she said. The main prize of a car, complete with concrete garage, was awarded at the end of the campaign after a televised draw was made by none other than Petula Clarke. The draw was made on a teatime TV news programme and, remarkably, the police were sent, lights flashing, to bring the winner, Miss Tomlinson, into the studio before the end of the show. Even more remarkably, and against all the odds, Miss Tomlinson was a TB sufferer herself. When asked if she was pleased with her prize Miss Tomlinson said that she was, though she planned to sell the car and buy a chesterfield settee and a holiday with the proceeds.

Below: This large scoreboard-style indicator was positioned at George Square and designed to track the progress of the various Glasgow districts towards the overall target in the TB campaign. Glasgow had been described as the TB blackspot of Europe, and the 33 day long campaign was intended to be the turning point in the battle against the disease. 50,000 posters had been displayed throughout the district to publicise the campaign, and the pages of every local and regional newspaper carried reports of how the campaign was being organised and managed. Metal badges were given to people after their X-ray had been carried out, and the whole city buzzed with excitement and curiosity as the major undertaking got underway. The Medical Officer of Health, Dr Horne, spearheaded the campaign and promised 1000 hospital beds for the worst cases identified in the operation. His aim was clear - to wipe out tuberculosis 'within our lifetime.' From an initial target of 250,000 X-rays over the five week period it soon became obvious that the number of people taking the test would surpass all expectations. After the first week the number of tests carried out was a staggering 142,000.

Bottom: Last minute queues at the end of the TB campaign resulted in most of the stations remaining open well after the scheduled closing time of 10.00 a.m. The crowds were so voluminous that the police had to be called in to keep order as the evening drew on. The George Square facility was open until midnight, the last X-ray being performed on Police Constable Robert Maxwell, aged 41, who was presented with a £5 voucher by Mr Bailie Mains, Convenor of the Health and Welfare Committee. Astonishingly, a total of 43,700 people had an X-ray on the final day of the campaign - making a total of 712,860 for the five week period. In all, a total of around 7,000 people had been found to be suffering from the disease, and the more serious cases were soon sent off to the allocated hospital beds for treatment. The X-rays found that some unlucky citizens had other chest problems; lung cancer and heart disease being the chief culprits. At the end of the campaign Dr. William A. Horne, the Chief Medical Officer of Health said that the end of TB was in sight.

On the move

Above: Large shops and stores which occupied corner positions on Glasgow's streets often liked to claim them as their own. On Charing Cross you could find Massey's Corner. Here, on Trongate, as it leads out to London Road, was Lawson's Corner. In case you weren't sure of Lawson's importance, the message was repeated as 'Lawson's of Glasgow Cross'. Further towards the bridge were Benson's and McEwan's. They were smaller concerns and contented themselves with just their names on the shop front. The London Road bridge in 1999 coincidentally carries an advert for MacEwan's beer. In the 1950s Glaswegians were being encouraged to buy Wills' Capstan cigarettes. There were no health warnings on tobacco adverts in those days. It is ironic to think that some of the city's wealth was due to the trade in the dreaded weed. Along this stretch of road the 18th century 'Tobacco Lords' would stroll, or strut, to be accurate. Cocky and proud of their importance, these merchants used to expect lesser mortals to move out of their way. Their influence declined rapidly as the end of the century approached, following the American War of Independence. Some place names, such as Virginia Street, keep those links with the old days of tobacco trading with the former colonies. The area around Glasgow Cross quickly became a rough and lawless place to be. The housing was just as bad and residents were amongst the unhealthiest in Glasgow, so insanitary were the living conditions.

Above right: McCann and MacKay's haulage contractor's van looks to be running in the tramtracks at Bridgeton. It might as well, because the trams won't be needing them. The distinctive tram shelter provides comfort and shelter for the two pensioners on the bench. Having spent a penny, though you go for free in the gents - always a source of annoyance for women, these men would be putting the world to rights. Maybe they were just discussing the fortunes of Motherwell or Partick Thistle soccer clubs, but it must be a riveting conversation. Their heads have not been turned by the mammoth £500,000 prize money on offer from Littlewoods Pools. This company was the brainchild of Liverpool's John Moores and became the major source of big prize money for punters in the 1960s. The National Lottery, scratchcards and the like would reduce this influence in the 1990s. Will former Dr Whos, like Tom Baker or Jon Pertwee, pop out of the police box in the corner? Behind the shelter of the Bridgeton Umbrella, the Olympia is showing 'A view from the bridge', the film of the Arthur Miller play about the Italian-American longshoreman whose passion for his niece leads to his downfall. Written in 1955 by the husband of Marilyn Monroe, this was a rather steamy subject for its time. The Olympia opened as the Theatre of Varieties in 1911. It became a cinema in 1924. Later, like so many others, bingo came here. By the 1990s, Full House Furnishings Ltd had arrived.

Below: Times change, but, then again, perhaps they don't. Small single decker buses carrying people in and out of the city had their day. All of a sudden, they are back with us. Private companies used to provide services in the 1920s. At the end of the century, with deregulation in force, they were back on the streets once more. Nippier and smaller than the double decker, they cause less congestion and keep traffic moving more smoothly. The 70 year old bus in the photograph looks as smart and gleaming as a new Dinky toy. An invisible hand only needs to pluck it off the street and place it on top of its display box to make the image complete. The driver is ready to set off on the western run to Paisley. The route followed a similar line taken by the M8 as it sweeps out beyond the home of the Thomas Coats Observatory. In 1937 the government sponsored the building of the large industrial estate that was home to some 150 factories. The demands on public transport to support the stream of workers out here meant fleets of buses and trams

ferrying them back and forth over the seven miles from the city centre. Our little bus couldn't have coped. The first motor bus had appeared in Glasgow in 1924, supplementing the trams. Corporation double deckers came in 1928 and provided stiff competition for the private companies. Garages and depots were established at Larkfield and Knightswood two years later.

Bottom: Carrying on into Woodlands Road, in the area now ripped apart by the motorway, the postwar trams trundle on towards Kelvinbridge and the west end, where a cosmopolitan mixture of small shops ply their trade today. At this end of the city there are a number of delightful terraces and sweeping crescents that mark out this part of Glasgow as a place of some elegance when it was in its pomp. The great houses were popular with well to do families, but became expensive to maintain. Many are now offices of one sort or another. In the 1950s, a variety of shopping and services could be had here, in the scene photographed. There was a tobacconist selling thick twist and rough shag, a place to repair your false choppers and somewhere to get your bread and fancy éclairs. The classy Vogue of London could kit you out in the latest fashion. This was Charing Cross Mansions, one of the few buildings around here to survive the ravages of the road planners. The Mansions date from 1891 and are an excellent example of late Victorian architecture. Built by JJ Burnet, they were later extended as Albany Chambers. They had been built on the site of the Georgian Albany Place. Burnet was an influential architect of the day. He was involved in the design of other important city buildings. His influence didn't end there. He showed his variety of ideas by assisting in the plans of the coachwork on the city's tramcars.

By the late 1950s the city centre was becoming a nightmare. It's probably Saturday and Lewis's and the other department stores are doing a good trade. The pavements are choc a block with shoppers. The streets are something else. The Hackney carriage would need more than just 'the knowledge' of destinations and addresses. He'd be well advised to have a fund of interesting stories to take passengers minds off the frustration of crawling along. The incident being attended to by the fire service hasn't helped, nor has the lorry in front. However, just look at the row of trams. Their inflexibility of movement, stuck to the tramlines as they were, slowed everything to a snail's pace. The increase in the number of private cars on the road had helped towards the mayhem. To improve

things, the days of the tram were numbered. It was not going to be possible to work round them. New roads into and out from the city were to come and the slum clearance programme and city regeneration had already begun. Whilst Glasgow had a comparatively low level of car ownership, the traffic flow needed restructuring. Trams were last to run in 1962. Trolley buses had been introduced in 1949, but these were tied to the overhead cable route and followed the trams out in 1967. The rail and bus services were improved. In 1960 the suburban electrified rail network was opened and one man-operated buses came a few years later. By the end of the 1990s, 39 per cent of all journeys are made on public transport, with four times as many people being carried on buses rather than by rail.

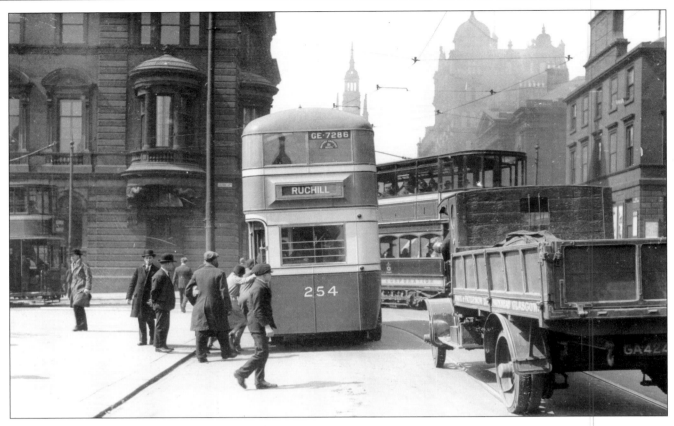

Above: Even back in the mid 20th century traffic congestion in the city was a major problem. The fumes and noise pollution of the large commercial vehicles, in particular, made the problems even worse. Jockeying for position between bus, tram, lorry and pedestrian was a tricky, slow and dangerous job. Referring to jobs, you could tell the sort each man had by his headgear. Nearly everyone wore a hat of some description, but the style was a give-away. The bowler hats belonged to those wheeling and dealing in the business sector. The flat hats or caps were for the working class and the trilby was sported by the in betweens, the pen pushers and minor civil servants. Scottish comedian, Ronnie Corbett, once performed an amusing sketch with Ronnie Barker and John Cleese. It described why he looked up to others of a higher class and why they looked down on him. The Ruchill bus is on its way to the part of the city that was once a series of merchants' country estates. At the time of this photograph, the company of Bryant and May, makers of Swan Vestas matches, was based at the old Ruchill Sawmills. To the left of the bus is George Square, with its monuments and statues of Glasgow's famous sons. Amongst many, they include Lt General Sir John Moore, James Watt, Thomas Campbell and Field Marshall Lord Clyde. Two proud stone lions stand by the Cenotaph, guarding the entrance to the municipal buildings of City Hall.

Above right: Great Western Road has always been a busy and dangerous highway. The little shopper needs to be very careful to look both ways before stepping out in front of the bus. The overtaking car is good evidence of the slogan once taught to children, 'Stop, look and listen'. Let's hope that advice is heeded, or any statistic is about to be recorded. McColl's fruiterer at the Botanic Gardens also specialised in wedding bouquets. Fresh fruit and flowers for sale. Many a young beau would stop here to buy a posy or a rose for his loved one. The popular Kenneth McKellar singing 'My love is like a red, red rose' might inspire later generations. The park and gardens behind led down to the River Kelvin and, with the exotic Victorian Kibble Palace in the background, were a romantic spot to be charmed by the attentions of the lad on your arm. One day a return visit might be made to order one of those bouquets for that most special of occasions. In the meantime, the Glassford Street bus waits for passengers from the station that was here from 1910 until it burned down in 1970. Whenever you see a six wheeler, how can you stop yourself humming the old Flanders and Swann song about the 97 horsepower omnibus? As long as singing it doesn't distract our young shopper, that's all right. Take care and that basket of goodies will get home safely.

The Scottish Daily Mail has the news that counts, or so it claimed around 1960. But what was going on here? It's around the time when prime minister Harold Macmillan had told us that we had never had it so good. People were packing the streets to try to prove him right, as shop cash registers started ringing again. The prosperity of the rest of Britain didn't reach Scotland to the same degree, but it was better than those first postwar years when austerity and rationing made us wonder who had really won the war. The revenue flowing in from the oilfields of the North Sea was yet to come ashore. Even when it did it didn't seem to do much more than make the fat cats fatter. Great matters of the economy were of little interest to these two boys. As long as they had their pocket money, they were content. A sherbet dip and a read of Roy of the Rovers in the Tiger lay ahead for them as they fingered the pennies in their fingers. Surely they are brothers. Mum seems to have had a good skein or two of wool and one pattern to work from. Oh for those days when boys had knees and little girls had white socks, even if they were a bit like Norah Batty's stockings. She doesn't look too happy on it, though. Perhaps she's been told that she can't have this week's Bunty. Whatever it is, she's going to enjoy a good sulk about it.

Bottom: It's the swinging 60s. The time of free love, flower power, Carnaby Street, Woodstock, Marmalade and the Beatles. Are these Glaswegians off to the Isle of Wight pop concert? That is stretching the imagination a little too far. A Saturday shopping expedition to the city centre is rather more likely. Money was a bit freer than in the early 50s. The attitude, now, was that a few extra shillings in the pocket needed spending in case the tighter times returned. Busy Ballater Street, with its nearby high rise flats, was a difficult place to cross in safety. The underpass cured that. Families didn't have to dodge the weekend traffic and could head off happily, shopping bags clutched tightly in hand. It was a family outing. Husbands and kids came along to escape the confines of the flats. Dad was helpful in carrying the bairns and opening his wallet to top up the house-keeping for the odd extra that caught our eye. He wasn't much use in the shops, getting under our feet as we tried to seek out a bargain or have a crack with the market trader or shopkeeper. He could be safely packed off for a quiet hour or two with his pals. On the way back, suitably warmed by a couple of pints of heavy, he might have mellowed enough to help carry the bags. You could always hope. The underpass was built by McKean & Company (Glasgow) Ltd. Coincidentally, the same firm would be commissioned to close it again. It was filled in with concrete in 1998.

Right: The new world and the old meet at Central Station. The trams, around in one form or another since the 1870s, pass one of the swish models of the day. The young man at the wheel of this 1960 Sunbeam was proud of his convertible. Sunbeam had attractive and racy sounding names for their cars. The 'Alpine' was one that had a real sporty

image. Anything that linked with Americans was also an enviable fashion item. Their music, hairstyles, clothing and movies were all the rage, or should one say 'hip'. today, they would be 'wicked'. Del Shannon singing 'Runaway', the Tony Curtis cut and this lad was in his element. Over to the right, Burton's tailors could be relied upon to provide the Saturday night suit. Casual dressing for a date or a dance was still on the horizon. The smart man was also a smoker. The Capstan medium cigarette was a popular brand. Those who tried the full strength variety, especially before breakfast, needed one strong head to remain standing! Our driver must have been brave to risk the Glasgow weather in baring his head to the elements. At least he was going under the place where people often used to congregate after church - the 'Hielanman's Umbrella' which carried the old Caledonian Railway. Duncan's Do'nut is now at the right of this photo and other fast food and amusement centres occupy premises nearby.

High days and holidays

The main entrance to Springburn Park was via the wide promenade of Broomfield Rd. It led to the bandstand and Winter Gardens. In the early years of the 1900s the middle class made their homes in this part of Springburn. Walking around there you would be rubbing shoulders with doctors, ministers, teachers and prosperous publicans. But when the sun shone and we headed off to the park, class was not a problem in the rowing boats on the lake. Nor did it matter to the children sailing their little home-made boats on the waters, keenly hanging on to the strings which they held in their hands. In the background a brass band would be playing to old men and women fast asleep in their deckchairs. In 1892, AB MacDonald, the City Engineer, laid out the 58 acres that the Corporation had bought for £25,000. A further 20 acres of New Mosesfield was added later. At its highest point the park is 351 ft above sea level. As Balgrayhill was so steep, it was the only Glasgow park that did not have a tram service right up to its gates. A year before his death in 1894, the respected industrialist James Reid donated the bandstand. A memorial to him was unveiled in 1903. On a fine day hundreds of locals would stroll around the lake or just sit in peaceful contemplation, looking quietly across its glassy surface.

Every city, in 1936, had its Locarno. The civil war in Spain and the rearming in Germany were a world away when, on a Saturday night, you could put on your glad rags and go up to Sauchiehall Street at Charing Cross and dance to your heart's content, or until the last bus or tram was due. If you were really lucky, there might be a nice, young chap to walk you home. If you were very lucky, a fish and chip supper on the way would be even better. Dancing to live bands is something the young of today know little of. Their grandparents danced holding each other! Fancy that, you youngsters! No jumping up and down on your own, being deafened by a headbanging row. For the 30s dancer there was a formula to each

dance. Slow, slow, quick-quick, slow and we were ready for the foxtrot. The more energetic had their moments, too. The jitterbug, the forerunner of the jive, had come from America and shocked the more staid dancer by its wild freewheeling. Still, there was always the last waltz to look forward to. There's a proper dance - a boy in your arms and your head on his chest. He'd sing in your ear the latest hit song, 'The way you look to-night', and you'd think how romantic he was. Little did you know he sang it in Molly McQueen's ear last week and it worked then as well! The Benny Daniels Orchestra continued to play here for many years after the war. The Locarno later became a casino.

Below: The four home countries used to play a round robin set of matches called the Home Championship. These finished in the 1970s when the hooligans won the day. After some scenes of crowd trouble, the series was scrapped. It was alive in 1970 when England visited Hampden Park. The reigning world champions used the game as a warm up for their defence of the title in Mexico, which was only a few weeks away. Scotland was anxious to send the Sassenachs off with their tails between their legs. It had a problem with its goalkeepers. Time and time again, the holder of the keeper's jersey had ended up being the butt of opponents' jokes. Remember the time of nine past Haffey? It wouldn't be until the late 80s and 90s, when Jim Leighton and Andy Goram came along, that the man between the sticks was admired. Around the time of this game Scotland was choosing Ferguson, Simpson,

Harvey and Herriott, amongst others. The latest to be tried was Jim Cruikshank of Heart of Midlothian. Jim was well respected by his fellow pros and supporters. However, he was unfashionable in not playing down south or for one of the Glasgow clubs. Seen cutting out one of the many crosses being thrown at him, he kept a clean sheet, denying the likes of Geoff Hurst and Martin Peters in a 0-0 draw. For some reason, the selectors didn't keep faith with him. He only won three caps.

Bottom: Hampden Park is the national soccer stadium. The home of Queens Park FC has seen many a famous match. In 1960 it hosted the European Cup Final. TV audiences across Europe thrilled to the skills of Eintracht of Frankfurt and Real Madrid. The Spanish champions, with such famous players as di Stefano and Puskas, won one of the best games ever seen, by seven goals to three. Over 135,000 were in the ground. However, it was when the 'auld enemy' came to play that the Hampden roar could be hear at its most ear splitting. Like a wall of sound, it rolled down from the terraces and across the park. To the Scottish team it was almost worth a goal start. Fans from rival clubs buried the hatchet for the day when England came to play. United in their common goal, they cheered on their heroes. In the 60s England had won the World Cup. That was of little significance to the Scot. Its only importance was if the English could be beaten. Then we could be regarded as unofficial world champions without the bother of playing through a tournament. Here, Celtic's 'wee jinky', Jimmy Johnstone, a star of the late 60s and 70s, comes up against Alan Ball. Although similar in stature, their style was totally different. Ball was a link man and dour tackler, whereas Jimmy loved to shimmy and trick his way round opponents. The Englishman was one of only two of the team of 1966 to become a successful manager.

Bird's eye view

Looking north across the Clyde and the city centre, in the foreground of this aerial view from about 1950, the sweep of the railway across the bridge and into Central Station stands out clearly. Also clearly prominent are the lines of commercial buildings and tenements that mark out Buchanan Street, Renfield Street, Blythswood Street, Newton Street and others. Glasgow has had a roller coaster of a population over the last two centuries, rising and falling quite dramatically. In 1800 there were but 77,000 people living here. By the time of World War I this had rocketed to six figures. The massive increase meant that there was both a housing shortage and tremendous overcrowding. Disease in these conditions was widespread: Glasgow was known as the tenement city. By the time the population peaked at over 1,100,000 at the start of World War II, most lived in one or two roomed tenement houses. These buildings were occupied from the cellars to the attics. Many of the lodging houses were more suited to pigsties than homes for humans. One resident of the time was quoted as saying that her husband didn't need to get out of bed in the morning to light the fire, so small was the house. In the 1940s and 1950s the City Council struggled to provide decent housing. In 1951 half of Glasgow's tenements had no inside bathroom and TB was rife. Major slum clearance schemes produced mixed results. Some regeneration merely produced modern high rise slums in the 70s.

The aerial view of the city shows the crowded and congested nature of Glasgow in the early postwar years. Probably dating from 1949, towards the left of this photograph Central Station can clearly be seen. The scene across the city, leading north from the river, has altered in the 50 years that have passed since this view. The first recognised centre of shopping in Glasgow developed in and around Glasgow Cross. In the 19th century, the commercial focus shifted west to the Sauchiehall Street/Argyle Street/Buchanan Street area, at the centre of this picture. The roads to be seen coming out of the city were lined with shops, above which large tenements loomed. The clearance of the inner city slums meant the loss of some traditional shopping areas. Some of the older ones, such as Springburn, Maryhill and Govan have been redeveloped. Glasgow is still the largest city in Scotland, boasting a population of over 600,000. However, this is only just over half of the peak figure of over 1,100,000 in 1939. The Bruce Plan of 1945 reduced housing densities and proposed new radial transport routes and industrial estates. There followed the Clyde Valley Regional Plan that took population and industry away from the centre. East Kilbride New Town and the estates at Castlemilk, Drumchapel and Easterhouse would be developed. By the end of the 20th century the city centre skyline would change to include the St Enoch Centre and the Buchanan Galleries. The latter opened in 1999 next to the Royal Concert Hall and is the largest in-centre shopping development in Scotland.

The writer, Daniel Defoe, spoke of Glasgow as a large well built city. He admired the grandeur of the stone buildings that made it one of the best and cleanest places in Great Britain. He was writing around 1700. At this time most Glaswegians lived around High Street and Saltmarket, The old town grew round the Cathedral, spreading gradually down to the Clyde. Defoe would have been referring to the large mansions that were developed on Buchanan Street, Queen Street and Virginia Street by the wealthy merchant class. What would he have said 250 years later? Life had changed dramatically in the period leading up to the time captured in his photograph. The Clyde had become as central to Glasgow's prosperity as it is to the photo. Steam driven weaving machinery had helped the cotton

and textile industry grow in importance and the ships of the Clyde gave easy access to overseas ports for both imports and exports. In one year alone, 105 million yards of American raw cotton were spun into thread. Some of it was taken down river and across the seas to India. Close links with America had been forged with the tobacco trade, which had made many men wealthy, the original 'Tobacco Lords'. The chemical industry grew around the textile business, supplying bleaches, dyes and stains for cloth. The 1798 St Rollox chemical works was one of the largest in Europe. Shipbuilding, which had been the new source of Glasgow's prosperity after the decline of the other industries, was about to experience its own slump as, captured in the aerial photograph, this particular day dawned.

Events & occasions

Central Station in the early 1900s is wall to wall with people. A few turn their heads upwards, having spotted the photographer snapping them. The advert for Sunlight soap seems appropriate. A crowded station is a mucky old place and a sweaty one, to boot. The railway lines were built at a low level, so the steam and grime from the locomotives had further to go to disperse. Many a tickle in the throat and many a soiled collar and cuff were the result of being in Central Station too long. Still, why not take heart from one of the other adverts and have a wee dram of Haig's to take your mind off the discomfort. It's not forever, though. today is Fair Saturday. Mid July and for two weeks we can forget our troubles. The factory workers

in the North of England have just finished their 'Wakes' holidays and now it's our turn. Trainloads of holidaymakers will descend on the Clyde coast to escape from the oppression of the city. Out will come the buckets and spades at Largs and Fairlie. Others would take the paddle steamers to Dunoon and Rothesay. More intrepid souls would venture further afield to the foreign shores of Blackpool and even the Isle of Man. That was continental for you. Ibiza and Majorca hadn't been invented yet. Who's to say our grandparents got any less fun from those days on our own coastline? Surely it compares with four hours on a plane to a place with warm beer and fish and chips we can get better at home?

Below: The canny Scot has a reputation for being careful with cash. Although the Citizen's story of counterfeit money in circulation caused concern, even the most careful wallet watcher knew what was the main story of the day. The 'caurs' were to move no more. It was an affectionate nickname for the tramcars that had carried millions of Glaswegians around the city. Nearly a century had gone by since the first one had moved out from St George's Cross. Now the death knell had sounded. The sight of trams, two and three abreast in their heyday, dominating the city streets were as much a part of Glasgow as the gondola is to Venice. Yet, the Council, in its wisdom, called time on another piece of tradition, consigning it to history. Destined for a final resting place in the Transport Museum, the Glasgow tram had lived to see six monarchs, two world wars and a development from horsepower to electricity. The last trams were large people carriers. The Coronation class of 1950 measured 35 ft by 7 ft and was 15 ft high. Weighing 16 tons, it transported 70 people. Congested streets and traffic gridlocks, with the rise in car ownership, meant a replanning of traffic flow and transport needs. The tram was sacrificed. From 1962 it trundled no more. The first ever journey had been made to Eglington Toll. The Tramway Theatre is on Eglington Street, keeping a connection with history.

Bottom: Although rationing is still around, the sense of deprivation has started to ease as 1952 draws to a close. There should be enough for a good spread at home when the relatives come to join us for Christmas lunch or a drink and a mince pie on Boxing Day. We can't go too mad, there's still Hogmanay to come and we'll need some supplies for that celebration. Still, those will be of a more liquid nature! In the meantime, there's the party at the recreation hall to enjoy. The members of the Salvage Corps, their wives and sweethearts, pose under the streamers and decorations ready to swap yarns, enjoy a dance, the odd silly game and a dram or two. They have earned their festive time together. One risks life and limb and the other isn't sure, when she hears the siren, of the level of danger her man is headed towards. We'll go daft in the head if we dwell on maybes, so let's put them out of our minds. Wind up the gramophone and put on a Jimmy Shand record and have a good old-fashioned party. The younger ones who want to dance to the latest pop sensation, Johnny Ray or whatever he's called, can wait. The Gay Gordons and an Eightsome Reel are the ones for a proper Christmas party. We can finish off with a game of musical laps, but I'll keep an eye on Hamish. If he tries it on with my Mary, like last year, he'll be wearing his teeth alongside his war medals, the season of goodwill or no.

Processions and parades have long been part of our national heritage. Some of them, particularly those proclaiming certain religious allegiances, have not always been accepted universally. However, there are no such problems with this one in Springburn Park. Hundreds gathered by the bandstand to watch the Temperance King and Queen lead the way across the lawns. The movement against alcohol abuse had long gathered force in Glasgow and many other large cities. Seeing the housekeeping blown in the bars had blighted too many lives. Fuelled by booze, men often became violent both in the home and on the street. The Saturday night punch-up was an all too common sight. The temperance movement tried to encourage family events as one way of distracting people from alcohol. The well scrubbed king doesn't look as though he'll grow up to be a tippler. He'll be in his 50s by now and be heartily sick of being teased about this shot from the family album. Less so the queen; for her it would remain a proud moment in her upbringing. The other little girls holding the train might be excused a little jealousy, but perhaps one of them would rise to the dizzy heights of royalty next year. Other walks in the 1950s that were popular included the Whit walk. Parading in a new set of clothes and collecting cash from assorted uncles and aunts was a feature of life in those days. The religious significance of the Whit festival was rather lost in the excitement of showing off your finery, like some pleased peacock. Despite that, wearing your Sunday best was important to us as a sign that work was done for the week and here was a particular day to be recognised.

On the home front

In the 1920s, the Glasgow Salvage Corps headquarters were to be found on Albion Street. Here, members of the corps sit proudly aboard two of their appliances. The Glasgow Corps was the last of three to be formed in the UK. The other two were in London and Liverpool. A number of fires in the city in the 1860s led the Insurance Committee to set up the Corps at its first station on Nicholas Street in 1873. There were eight full-time members with just one horse drawn trap. These men worked as an organisation independently of the fire brigade. Their job was to reduce the amount of damage and loss in a fire, so reducing hardship and helping business resume as soon as possible. Obviously, this saved the insurance companies money. The main problem was water damage, not the fire itself. The salvagemen would often work in pairs. Having weighed up the situation in the premises, stock, furniture and equipment would be sheeted in such a way as to divert water from the hosepipes. Water would also be diverted towards suitable exit points. The first superintendent was Edwin Goodchild, who held the position until his death in 1887. Around this time, the Corps moved to the station on Albion Street, from where it operated until 1972.

At first, some members of the regular fire service mistrusted the Corps, believing it would hamper firefighting. The efficiency of Mr Goodchild and the bravery of his men changed those ideas and a mutual respect developed.

Below: 'They shall grow not old, as we that are left grow old. Age shall not weary them, nor the years condemn.' The words of Laurence Binyon that are spoken at every Remembrance Day service up and down the land each year. Although meant to commemorate the fallen in the two world wars, the service acts as a focal point of remembrance for all who have made the ultimate sacrifice in the defence of others. Included in our thoughts on the second Sunday in each November are those brave police and fire officers who perished helping others, as well as members of the armed forces in such conflicts as Malaya, the Falklands and the Gulf. Here, in the 1960s, William Noddings, Ronald Bevan and Peter Gilligan prepare to pay their tribute by laying the Salvage Corps wreath at the War Memorial. Being in uniform, it is quite proper that they wear their hats. Civilians, to a man, will have removed theirs out of respect.

On the day of this photograph, there will have been many veterans from the second world war paying homage to old comrades. Those who fought in the Great War are, by now, pensioners, but they will turn out, come what may. By the end of the century, hardly a single soldier from the Somme will remain. However, 'at the going down of the sun and in the morning, we will remember them.'

Bottom: This jolly group of men is celebrating the move of the Salvage Corps headquarters from Albion Street to the new centre on Maitland Street in April 1972. This had the unusual effect of locating Fire, Police and Ambulance services within a few yards of each other. The salvagemen are striking a more relaxed pose than seen in pictures of their predecessors. Portraits taken in earlier days were always stuffily staged. Albion Street had been home since the mid 1880s. The new headquarters was only to be theirs for another 12 years, when the Corps would cease operations. All three of the country's Salvage Corps were wound up in 1984. Some of the men joined the Brigade, but most accepted redundancy. Maitland Street became a general Strathclyde Brigade training centre. In the final years, the work continued to be demanding. In 1973 there were 2,854 call outs. However, by 1982 the number of attendances at fires had fallen to 1,300. Britain wasn't alone in its Salvage Corps. Similar Corps or Fire Patrols existed throughout America. There is even one in Bombay. This was begun in 1907 and now specialises in advising in training firefighters and salvage workers in the textile and other industries. This is a reminder that the work of our Corps was not just in attending fires. Remembering the links with insurance, members would patrol warehouses covered by the Insurance Companies. Advice on fire prevention and storage methods was given. Suggestions were made on the design of warehouses, so incorporating such features as inclines for water drainage and stairways which led directly to outside doors.

Both pictures: The power of fire and the total disregard for anything in its way was brought home to the people of Glasgow that horrid day on 28th March 1960. About 20,000 barrels of whisky and other spirits were thought to have been held in a six storey bonded warehouse in Cheapside. Fire had been reported in a neighbouring building and Granston Street Fire Station crew attended, accompanied by the Salvage Corps. Within the hour, the fire had taken hold and spread quickly. Without warning, a huge explosion ripped out the sides of the warehouse. Flames, fuelled by the thousands of gallons of whisky, soared high in the sky. Fourteen fire service personnel and five salvagemen were killed. It took 36 hours to recover the final body. Glasgow had seen major fires before. Those at Grafton's Fashions and the furniture store of Leon & Co had claimed lives, but no-one was prepared for a disaster on this scale. The city was stunned. Princess Margaret visited, to pay the respects of the Royal Family. Services were held at Glasgow Cathedral and St Andrew's Cathedral. Fire crews from all over Britain sent a contingent to share the city's loss. The Lord Provost launched a disaster appeal that raised £180,000. Two firemen were awarded the George Medal and three others the British Empire Medal. The solemn men in the photograph are attending the dedication of the plaque on Albion Street to the Salvage Corps men who perished that sad day. 'The name of Cheapside will forever bear a hallowed place in the history of the city of Glasgow, recording the supreme sacrifice of so many fine and courageous firefighters.'

IN MEMORY OF
THE OFFICER & MEN
OF GLASGOW SALVAGE CORPS
WHO LOST THEIR LIVES
IN THE DISASTROUS FIRE
CHEAPSIDE STREET GLASGOW
28TH MARCH 1960

SUPT. E. C. MURRAY
L/S/M. J. A. McLELLAN
S/M. W. OLIVER
S/M. J. F. MUNGALL
S/M. G. C. McMILLAN

Above: During World War II, the Glasgow Salvage Corps placed itself at the disposal of the city for firefighting duties. However, the salvage role was deemed more important and Corps members trained Fire Service members in salvage methods. The Auxiliary Fire Service had been formed in 1938, but all brigades were absorbed into the National Fire Service three years later. After the big air raids on Coventry and other English cities, Glasgow trained hard for what was, inevitably, to come its way. In September, 1940, bombs fell on Partick, Yoker and Yorkhill. A 250 lb bomb at Yorkhill quay hit the 10,000 ton cruiser Sussex and 2,000 residents were evacuated. However, this was nothing compared to the blitz on Clydeside in March 1941. Only a dozen houses escaped without damage. Further attacks during the year stretched the resources of the fire and salvage services. This two ton Austin K2 wagon, with its 30 ft ladder, was added to the fleet in 1942. It was used to pull various pumps, water tanks etc as and when required. The addition of radio communication in the cabs improved the speed and

efficiency of reaction to any new incident. The badge of the Corps was displayed on its side. As well as the city coat of arms, the shield contained the wall, wave lines and flames. These represented the main elements of the salvagemen's work. The wall was for protection, the wave lines for water and the flames for fire.

Top: Bridgeton Cross is out along the London Road at the east end of the city. Parkhead, the home of Celtic Park where Glasgow Celtic plays its soccer matches is only a short distance away. The ornate tram shelter was both functional and an architectural delight. These structures were dotted along the tram routes and this one has been preserved as a living part of Bridgeton today. The police box for emergency use was a common feature on our streets, even in the 1960s. They are now best remembered as the home of the Tardis, the space and time ship of the TV character Dr Who. Played originally by William Hartnell, we all remember the exploits of the eccentric Doctor and his battles with those most frightening of enemies, the Daleks. Most children watched from the safety of the rear of the sofa, peeking over the back in excited terror at the mechanical monsters. Sadly, the box has long gone from Bridgeton. In this district you could have found some of the worst housing in the country, never mind just Glasgow. In 1870 here were some 30 tenements, each containing 16 different households. Living conditions were filthy. Open middens were only a part of the insanitary conditions, as disease ran unchecked. The city population increased dramatically, rising from 250,000 in 1841 to over 1,000,000 by the end of the century. Highlanders, Irish fleeing from famine and Eastern European Jews escaping persecution all added to the overcrowding in this poverty stricken area.

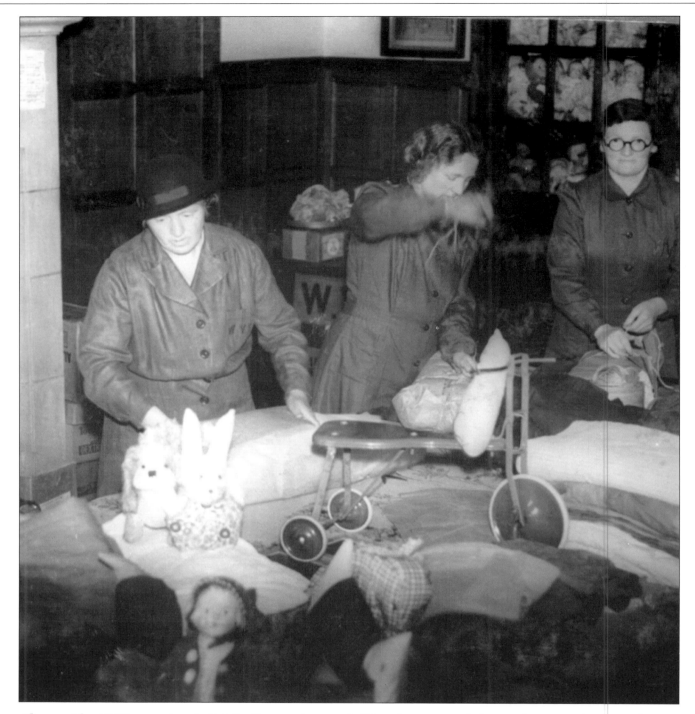

Above: The WVS appeal and distribution centre had organised salvage collections for the RAF. Aluminium pots and pans, kettles, saucepans, jelly moulds and colanders were gathered from Glasgow homes and around. From the first such collection over 1,000 tons of metal salvage was realised. It was heartening to think we had contributed to that Spitfire protecting our skies, though it was difficult to believe it was some form of flying frying pan! In this photograph, the sorting mainly concentrates on the toys and clothes that have been gathered. Some lucky toddler will soon be whizzing around on that trike. But what about those bunnies! The ears certainly have it. You don't need much imagination to see a child whooping with glee at getting such a lovely present. Bugs Bunny himself couldn't hope to rival those grand pairs of 'jug handles'!

Elsewhere around the sorting area there was box upon box labelled 'milk tops', 'bones', 'paper', 'pig food' etc. Nothing that was of possible use or that could be recycled was discarded. 'What can you do?' asked ARP posters at the beginning of the war. More women than men responded by volunteering their services as Air Raid Wardens. However, given little to do, they drifted off. Happily, many were then recruited by the WVS. Then, they certainly found plenty to occupy them, valuably and usefully, too. Responding to the needs of others was a true war effort. When Lord Woolton (he of the revolting pie) appealed for blankets, the WVS was there to organise. When the residents of Coventry cried out for help after their city's blitz, the Glasgow Women's Voluntary Service was there to co-ordinate relief.

Right: The war effort wasn't all about scavenging metal for new warplanes. There were any number of appeals for clothing and toys for displaced and unfortunate families. Here WVS members are surrounded with items collected or sent in to help those who were in need. The WVS became an official clothing distribution centre for Glasgow Corporation. The Post Office would provide the transport and delivery of the results of the appeal and the women would then leap into action. The dollies would bring joy to the hearts of little girls whose homes had been flattened by the 1941 Clydeside blitz and those of later Luftwaffe raids. The little lassie who would get one of these dolls as a gift to replace the one she had lost would gain much comfort from it. It would be something to cuddle and gain comfort from was.

Below: Purposefully striding out on their way to a church service, these ladies of the Women's Voluntary Service celebrate the fifth anniversary of its formation. Sensible shoes and a sturdy uniform typify the resolve of these women. Theirs was a practical role, born of the necessity of wartime. This wasn't a group of well meaning middle class women holding coffee mornings and chatting about the war effort. They did something about it. It was the army that Hitler forgot. By July 1943 they had much of which to be proud. Air Raid Precaution had slowly been developed during the 1930s and the WVS was founded in 1938 as a support to the ARP. People remembered the valuable and vital work women had done in World War I, when so many traditional and difficult male roles had come their way whilst the men were in the trenches.

Above: On the hotline to Churchill? Whoever she was talking to, the WVS member on the right wouldn't have been chatting idly. Pencil in hand, she was seeking important information to help others passing through Central Station in May 1944. The soldiers leaning through the hatches came to rely on the help these women could give them in finding their way across the country. As well as the British, many soldiers from overseas, Poles, Free French, Americans and Canadians, passed through Central Station on their way to new billets or off on a short leave. The WVS assumed the role of guides or information officers. These Glasgow guides were to meet every troop train, day or night, throughout the war. Many a Tommy would pretend to need a personal escort from a younger Service member to find his way across the city, but she had heard all the lines before. A sweet smile and a knowing look was the only response he was likely to get. Still, you couldn't blame him for trying. The two lads on the left won't get much change out of the woman they're speaking to. She looks as though she could eat them for breakfast. There were times when you needed to be forceful and resilient in the WVS. The first bomb that fell on Britain landed on a WVS house in the Orkneys in February 1940! One member single-handedly captured a German parachutist in Yorkshire. She led him, on the end of her pitchfork, to the local police station where the flier was happy to be locked up in safety.

Right: In 1940, the mobile emergency feeding canteen appeared on Glasgow streets. Men had become used to seeing women driving ambulances, lorries and vans during the Great War, so there was little sexist objection to the woman behind the wheel of the canteen. Certainly there wasn't from these chaps. The Women's Voluntary Service gave support when there were food supply problems, something that was to become more important as the war continued. After a fire or a bombing, the canteen would arrive with a warm meal and hot drink to give refreshment to the emergency services and feed those who had been driven from their homes. Before the coming of the welfare state, these women acted as an unofficial social service, supporting deprived families in the run-down parts of Glasgow where poverty and unemployment were a way of life. Stella, Lady Reading, had formed the organisation. She had been at the heart of the Personal Service League of the early 30s that helped families adversely affected by the depression years. Born Stella Charnaud, in 1894, in Constantinople, she brought her cosmopolitan, but social, conscience to the front line of helping the unfortunate. After her husband's death in 1935, she immersed herself in charitable projects. The WVS was formed in 1938 and Lady Reading became its first chairman. Recognising that war was coming, the WVS organised first aid and gas defence classes for civilians. These women ran trolley shops in hospitals and cared for the relatives of men who were on the danger list. Their later work in wartime would see a number of them appear on the same danger list.

Left: During World War II the WVS helped co-ordinate the evacuation of refugees from Glasgow. Unlike the rest of the country, which shipped people in large groups of mothers, teachers, children and escorts, the city's children were usually evacuated just with their mothers. Some 42 per cent of Glasgow's children moved out, although many returned before too long. Being homesick was worse than the risk of being bombed. Children being evacuated were given a good inspection, particularly of the hair. Reading about it now brings back memories of Nitty Nora, the school nurse. 'A louse is not a political creature; it cannot distinguish between the salt of the earth and the scum of the earth.' So there! By the time of this photograph, 1953, the WVS had developed the Meals on Wheels service which had been established in 1948. It was a tanner for a main dish and tuppence for a pudding. Here an emergency feeding demonstration is taking place at Crookston Homes. Three Glasgow MPs and a large contingent of councillors attended. There were improvised hot plate ovens, built with bricks, oil drums and waste materials that could be made large enough to feed 500 people.

By 1961, Baroness Swanborough, then chairman of the WVS, spoke in the House of Lords, 'to call attention to the need for an extension of the meals on wheels scheme in the care of the housebound. Local authorities should be authorised to provide kitchens etc for voluntary bodies.' The WVS also ran a home help service. By 1950, 44 out of the 55 Scottish local authorities had such a service.

Above: The work of the WVS attracted many sponsors, such was the high regard in which the Service was held. This van was presented by the Trades Houses of Glasgow. The women who were the rank and file had become considered to be a vital wing of the Civil Defence. They were also an official outlet of the Ministry of Food. They would leap into action at the centre of any emergency, serving soup, sandwiches and food until local emergency feeding arrangements came into force. As more modern times arrived, the WVS (from 1966 WRVS) spread its wings into other aspects of social need. Some became hospital phone and radio operators, whilst others involved themselves in organising activities and outings for the kiddies in children's homes. A home for ex-Borstal boys was established in the city in November 1963. The house was made available by the Corporation, a further sign of the recognition of the worth of the work of the WVS. The home became a sort of halfway house. It gave the boys a breathing space between the institution and the outside world. They were helped to find decent lodgings and encouraged to look for worthwhile jobs, rather than just turned loose to return to the streets from which they had come. The Service also went into prisons, giving life classes to prisoners prior to their release, hopefully equipping them with skills to cope with the world they would meet outside.

By the time of this 1940 view of the WVS mobile canteen, Queen Elizabeth (now the Queen Mother) had become the Service's president, thus giving royal approval of the work being done. This became official in 1966 when it became the WRVS, the Women's Royal Voluntary Service. The canteen had been presented by the Scottish Iron and Steel Scrap Association. As well as giving out food to the deprived, after the first large bombing raids on our cities in World War II the canteens developed through and after the hostilities as support vehicles in times of major disasters. There were to be food convoys for the disaster areas, 18 Queen's Messenger Convoys being developed - a sort of food flying squad. This was a far cry from the humble harvesters' pie

scheme started in the early days of the war. The horrific floods on the East coast of England in 1953 brought out the WVS in force. It is a poignant fact that a few weeks after adding the 'Royal' to its title, the Service would be attending the event which hurt us all in October 1966 - Aberfan. This Welsh village lost 112 children and 28 adults to a slag heap slide. From then, disaster response training would be part and parcel of the training of the Glasgow WRVS. At the height of its wartime work the Service had around 1,000,000 members throughout Britain. Hitler had more than the troops at the front with whom to contend. Being out and about helping others was not without its dangers. Between 1941 and 1944, some 241 WVS women lost their lives to the bombs.

Down at the docks

What a racket. People cheering and waving on the quayside is bad enough, but the din on board is phenomenal. Hundreds of high-pitched voices, chattering, laughing and squealing with delight; it's a threat to the eardrums. The paddle steamer Eagle III is leaving Broomielaw in 1929 on an outing. The occasion is a special one as it's a trip for the children from the Quarrier's Home. To make it even more special, this was the centenary year of the birth of the founder of the homes, William Quarrier. His homes have sometimes been called the Scottish Barnardo's. Quarrier, however, had little in the way of the sort of public high profile Barnardo enjoyed. He sought little in public or private funding and, consequently, the advertising of his service to the unfortunate and needy is minimal. William

Quarrier was born into a poor family, but became wealthy as a self-made businessman with a string of shoe shops. Perhaps he pulled himself up by his own bootlaces! Touched by the plight of a poor, young match-seller he saw in the East End of Glasgow, he opened his first home for such wretches in Renfrew Lane in 1871. He preferred to take in orphans, believing that those with parents should first look to their own family. Helping them find their way in life, Quarrier assisted many to start anew in Canada. Sixteen miles from the city is the village that was built to get away from the dormitories and workhouse style of other orphanages. It is, possibly, from this village that the excited hordes have come on this day to go 'doon the watter' and have a day to remember.

The Sailors' Home, from where this photo was taken, was a hostel at 150 Broomielaw. Bought at a cost of £12,000 in 1856, it was extended in 1906. The decline of Glasgow as a major port after World War II led to its demolition in 1971. Seen from the old Sailors' Home, with its round tower and time ball, the George V Bridge was built at a height of 18 ft above the high water level. This let small coasting vessels pass under it on their way to and from Broomielaw. In the 19th and early 20th centuries, this section of the river would have been a highway of shipping sailing between the lines of the quays. Transatlantic steamers of the Anchor, Allan and Donaldson lines provided regular services taking emigrants to the United States and Canada. Cargo steamers brought in food for the growing population and sailed out again, loaded with

pig iron, coal and machinery. John Masefield's poem, 'Cargoes', could well be adapted to refer to these. 'Dirty British coaster with a salt-caked smokestack'. Looking across the Broomielaw sheds and beyond the bridge, the city centre businesses carry on their trade, knowing that access to the markets of the world can be gained from the Clyde quayside a short distance away. To the right are the fringes of the much criti-cised district of the Gorbals. Ever since the 50s this area has been subject to demolition, development and then more of the same. The bridge names of George V, Victoria and Albert provide a link with the past. Will they stay for the future, as greater devolution comes to Scotland? Perhaps there'll be the King Duncan or Macbeth Bridges. Heaven help us if we get Blair or Dewar Bridge!

So you thought the M8 and A74 into the city were busy, did you? Rush hour, with its curse of bumper to bumper traffic and frustrated souls snarled up in long jams, is the scourge of the commuter of the modern era, isn't it? Think again. Better still, look again at this scene and its date. The year is 1924. On Jamaica (Glasgow) Bridge hardly a square inch of road surface is to be seen. Goodness knows how many hundreds or even thousands of people are being carried across the water at this one time frame in our history. Bridges, as the only real form of river crossing, were always going to be a busy focus for travellers. However, no-one in 1767, when the first stone for the original structure was laid, could have envisaged such a volume of use a century and a half later. Also confusingly known to some as Broomielaw Bridge and, in its early days as Bonny Brig, it had opened in 1772. A marvel of engineering of that age, it measured 500 ft in length and 32 ft in width. Its seven arches spanned Glasgow's life-blood, the Clyde. It had distinctive circular holes, or ox-eyes, to carry off surplus floodwater. However, it was hump backed and unable to cope with an increase in traffic, even in those days. So, reconsider your opinion of modern urban motoring. Previous generations suffered before you were even thought of. Perhaps they coped with the frustrations better. Road rage is an invention of today's society. Our forebears had that wee bit more tolerance, or so granddad always says.

Below: The change in Glasgow's prosperity has never been more marked than in the changing fortunes of the shipyards. Govan docks. In 1966, the Geddes Report said that there were insufficient grounds, whether it be for social reasons or to bolster the balance of payments, to continue to build a lot of ships. It concluded that it might be better to let the industry decline. This sounded the death knell for yards on the Clyde. It was the beginning of the end of a way of life that drove trades union activists like Jimmy Reid to the front pages of the national papers. Remember the work-in of 1971 at Upper Clyde Shipbuilders when the government decided to force it into liquidation? It was all a far cry from the halcyon days of years ago. In 1864, London & Glasgow Shipbuilding and Engineering opened at Govan. Harland & Wolff took over in the early 1900s and built the world's largest ship, the Olympic. The company also erected the nearby tenements for its workers. As an employer of Protestant leanings, Harland & Wolff was indirectly responsible in supplying ardent Protestant supporters for the Glasgow Rangers soccer team. Between 1860 and the start of World War I over one third of all British shipping was built on Clydeside. From the building of the first steam powered ships in the early 19th century to the steel built ones at the end of the century, the Clyde led the world. Yards here, at Partick and Scotstoun built them all, from yachts to cargo vessels, from warships to submarines.

Bottom: Here we're viewing Jamaica Bridge from Carlton Place, on the south side of the river. By the summer of 1936, a variety of public and private transport was crossing the Clyde. The river, as much as the volume of traffic, had been responsible for the building of various bridges at this crossing place. Water erosion had made the 18th century bridge unstable, even within not much more than half a century of its opening. Its replacement was twice as wide. It is recorded that, in the first week of its opening in 1866, over 20,000 pedestrians, 253 horse-riders, 160 carriages, 634 carts and 166 wheelbarrows passed across its seven arches. Designed by the famous Thomas Telford of Dumfries, just before his death in 1834, it had been a long time in the coming. Unfortunately, despite the pedigree of its designer, it was a short time in the replacing. Having taken 33 years from foundation stone to opening, it took the same time to the introduction of the third and latest bridge. Telford's bridge had been too narrow, despite having been almost double the width of the one it replaced. The arches were also too close together to allow larger vessels to pass through them. The current bridge has, though, kept some of the hallmarks of Telford's trade. The granite facings, balustrades and copings were all reused. Remember saving the 'divvy' stamps from the Co-op, as reminded by the advert on the railway bridge? Begun in the little street of Toad Lane in Rochdale, Lancashire in 1844, it became an international retail and wholesale trade organisation, its profits being redistributed to its members. The SCWS had its headquarters in Morrison Street.

Down at the shops

The car turning at the crossroads between Argyle Street and Jamaica Street clearly dates this photograph. It's a troubled era in America. You can almost see Eliot Ness and the Untouchables jumping on to the running board and chasing Al Capone down the street, machine guns blazing. No such uproar in the Glasgow of 1930. Shopping is the order of the day, not prohibition. God help the politician who tried to introduce that piece of legislation here! Argyle Street was once a two mile stretch from Trongate to the Kelvin. The M8 motorway has now bisected it and the street disappears for a while around Anderston, before reappearing further west. Back in the 1820s, the architect, John Baird, designed the 480 ft dog-leg of the Argyle Arcade. Influenced by London's Burlington Arcade, Glasgow's answer was a number of top establishments, which later mainly concentrated upon the jewellery trade. Back in the early days such outlets as Galetti's sold mirrors and optical glasses, but later diversified into model yachts, steam engines and locomotives around the turn of the century. Here, the scene is of Simpson's Corner, with the name of Robert Simpson proudly displayed on the Jamaica Street awnings. Round the corner, on Argyle Street, is the place of many an ill spent youth, the billiard hall. The goods at One Price, lower right, turn the heads of the man pushing the barrow. What did he fancy for 16s 9d? These days, the eastern end of the street is dominated by the St Enoch Centre, sometimes known as the Great Greenhouse because of the huge amount of glass in the structure.

Above: Glasgow is hillier than you think. Sitting in a two litre car, speeding along the expressway that is now Springburn Road, it is difficult to imagine struggling up the hill towards Balgrayhill, to the north in this picture. That was our lot 40 or 50 years ago. Carrying the shopping, pushing the pram or cycling were hard work. It wasn't called the 'push bike' for nothing. Back in the 1920s and 1930s, this was a popular area for photographs to be taken for the picture postcard industry. The building that has the clock on its gable was Quin's. It was a favourite pub with drinkers and photographers. Sometimes they were the same! Quin's had a small bar and games room. The click of dominoes and the shuffling of the cards for games of crib, don and pontoon were sounds common to all bars where men gathered. Heaven help the woman who invaded the working man's retreat. She'd only interrupt once. Under the stairs was a small toilet, known, for obvious reasons as the 'wee' room. There was a tram shelter in front of the bar. This was very useful for those who had one too many. They could be poured out of the pub and straight onto the tram to take them home. The other main drinking spot was Gemmell's (later Kelvin's). The church to the right is Wellfield United, built in 1899. It joined others in 1978 to become Springburn Parish Church. All that is left now is the Barclay Street tenement on the top of the hill.

Above right: Don't be fooled by the name on the building by the traffic light. 'Edinburgh Warehouse 30 Princes Street' is tricking you into believing for a moment that you've suddenly slipped eastwards to that city on the Firth of Forth. Calm down! You're still in Glasgow, just across the way from Central Station. At the corner of Gordon Street and Renfield Street, Saxone's was claiming the corner for itself. 'Saxone for men' wasn't the Viagra of 40 years ago, but a suggestion that the shop could supply your footwear better than most. Dolcis, further along on the right, probably disagreed. Crocodile leather shoes and winkle pickers were in vogue. Dad wasn't convinced. He 'couldna get his tootsies in those things' was how he put it. The shoe shops had their origins in the leather industries of Victorian times. As well as belting for machines, companies widened their horizons to include the manufacture of boots and shoes. Martin's of Bridgeton was well known for the footwear it provided for soldiers in the first world war. The Scottish Co-operative Society also had a particularly fine reputation for the quality of its goods. The sleek lines of the 'limo', following its more mundane colleagues over the cobbled sets, was a reminder of the days when British motors, like the Jaguar, were the envy of the world, winning sports car events and a number of Monte Carlo rallies. It stands out grandly in its more humble company. Perhaps the driver was a tourist.

Below: Roll up, roll up! The great sale is now on. Discounts for everyone. Don't you tire of those TV adverts for the great discount stores which offer furniture sales etc that must end on Sunday? The only trouble is, the very same advert appears next week and the week after and the week after .... But it's not just a phenomenon of the 1990s. Forty years ago (and more) they were at it, albeit in a more restrained fashion. The man in the sandwich board was a cheap way to get the message around town. You couldn't miss him as he, rather miserably, ambled up and down the road, hoping the rain would keep off. Auntie Wainwright, in TV's 'Last of the summer wine', used much the same sort of person in Smiler, played by Stephen Lewis. He,

forlornly, traipsed around trying to drum up custom for her and his character was based on one such as the fellow pictured here. To-morrow might see him with a different set of boards. 'The end is nigh' or 'Repent ye all sinners' were other messages to be carried along the cobblestones. Who took any notice? But they carried on doing so, anyway. Unfortunately, most people seem to be ignoring the message of the Argyle Warehouse. There's Marks and Spencer's department store to be visited, instead. Perhaps the sandwich board carrier can say a prayer to St Michael that we leave and follow him from there to Virginia Street.

Bottom: Looking north towards Balgrayhill, the tram is twisting and winding its way along Springburn Rd before taking its route out to the west. Although old Springburn has disappeared, across from the florist's, there are still some tenements standing in between Kay Street and Carleston Street. There are also refurbished ones along Keppochill Rd. The conditions inside them are a far cry from those suffered by our grandparents. The Kay Street baths have gone. Amazingly, the new sports centre built on the old recreation ground lacked a swimming pool. A large shopping centre now occupies the site to the right. You can get what you want under one roof. It may be convenient, but it lacks the character and atmosphere of going in and out of the smaller shops which had their own specialities and catered for individual needs. You were known personally to the shopkeeper, who always greeted you like a long lost friend. We had time to ask about each other's health and family. Even Auntie Jean's back problems became a source of concern and animated discussion. In the shopping centre you're just a number or a wallet to be opened. The tram will soon pass the corner at Cowlairs. Railway workers will be getting off for their next shift at the North British Locomotive Co Ltd works. The company was formed when three engine builders, Dubs, Reid and Stewart, joined forces in 1903.

It's a fine day in Glasgow city centre. In St Enoch Square, looking north towards Buchanan Street, shoppers merrily move from the shoe shop at Trueform, past H Samuel's jeweller's, at the MacDonald Argyle Street frontage, to Montague Burton's store. The proper full Monty (a suit of clothes) could be bought here. The Tardis wouldn't survive much longer. It belonged to a bygone age, as it was now 1976. The flared trousers of the younger generation crossing the square contrast with the old-fashioned garb of the women in front of the police box. Denims and tailored jeans became the fashion for both sexes. In trousers and with the fashionable long hair, from a distance it was difficult to tell men and women apart. This led to more than one rather embarrassing encounter. St Enoch Square goes back to the 1770s. There used to be a church at its heart, but that disappeared in 1925. By the time pictured, the dramatic listed building of St Enoch Station and its Hotel were soon to be swept away. The station had terminus of the old LMS line. Abba was topping the pop charts and 'Save your kisses for me' was winning the Eurovision Song Contest. Mrs Thatcher had been the Tory leader for just a year. Change was just around the corner. It would help pave the way for he building of new centres that altered the style of shopping in our cities. The St Enoch Centre was to open in 1989.

Above: Coming towards us is the No 37 to Castlemilk. Its journey from here on Springburn Rd takes it to the south of the city, out beyond Rutherglen. This area, around Vulcan Street and Cowlairs Rd, was known as Springburn Cross. It is now totally unrecognisable, as the demolition and regeneration of the later part of the 20th century has torn down most of what you see. The new expressway and motorway, added to the shopping centre and modern housing has destroyed the character of Springburn. In the 50s, this was a busy little spot, a community in its own right. Going back to the end of the 18th century, it was a village that was home to weavers, farm labourers and men who worked in the quarries. Nearby, there was farmland and many of Glasgow's richer merchants had their country homes around here. The coming of the age of rail changed all that. Within 50 years the Edinburgh and Glasgow Railway would run through Springburn and the railway workshops would be sited at Cowlairs. Before too long, this would be to locomotive building what Govan was to the ship building industry. Population increased quickly and better paid jobs for workers in the locomotive industry took men from the land and traditional work. Homes were built and the cramped and condensed district of Springburn was reborn as an example of Victorian industry and housing. The retail trade soon followed and the Cross was the heart of an almost self-contained satellite of Glasgow.

Right: Everybody outside Glasgow knows about the city's main street: Sauchiehall Street. This, though, is just not true. To the native, Buchanan Street was the one that held pride of place as a shopper's paradise. If you want any further proof, just look at what's happening in 1948 as you look south from the eastern end of Sauchiehall Street. This is a time of austerity, remember. The ration book is still needed to buy clothing, food and petrol. Yet, the street is teeming with people and cars, both burning money in their different ways. Buchanan Street always has been that little bit special. today cars are banned completely. You can walk and window shop in the pedestrian area, safe in the knowledge that no wildly driven Morris Cowley is going to make you jump back on to the pavement. Can you spot what had been banned in this earlier era? Look carefully and you will come to realise the absence of the main feature of any Glasgow street during the first half of the 20th century - the tramcar. Of all the important ones, Buchanan Street was the only one to resist the pressure of those who wanted to lay tracks for the vulgar tram along its length. Before the motor-car crowded the road, the absence of the tram helped Buchanan Street retain an air of superiority as a centre of quality and value. Formed in the 18th century, it first became important for its luxury department stores. Here, shops such as H Samuel's jeweller's, Burton's tailor's, Lizar's optician's and the Clydesdale Bank (now the Bradford & Bingley) illustrate the variety offered to the shopper of the time.

At work

Between the two world wars, the north side of the river bank, from Glasgow Bridge to the River Kelvin, was developed for shipping. On the south side, quays lined the banks to Govan, before further quays took shipping to the west of Glasgow. You could see dry docks, cranes and every modern assistance to shipping and trade. Despite government orders for ships, the industry started to fall away after World War I. This accelerated after World War II. Competition from Sweden, Germany and Japan saw off Clydeside. Attempts to modernise in the 1930s were a failure and by the 1990s only two shipyards remained. One of Glasgow's best known shipyards was John Brown's, seen here in 1956. These could be monsters from a futuristic War of the Worlds. Just as Manhattan has its skyscrapers, so Clydeside had its huge crane derricks. James and George Thomson started the business in 1847 as a marine engineering concern at the Clydebank Foundry. A shipyard was opened at Govan in 1851 and built the paddle steamer Jackal the following year. Other notable ships were Jura (1854) and Russia (1867), both built for Cunard. After moving to Clydebank, the City of Paris and the City of New York were built for Inman Lines. In 1892 HMS Ramillies was completed. John Brown, a Sheffield steel company took over the yard in 1899. The business was modernised and flourished, with the help of large Admiralty and merchant contracts. The ill-fated Lusitania was built for the Cunard line. It was torpedoed with a large loss of civilian life in 1915. John Brown's also built HMS Hood, which was sunk by the Bismarck in 1941. However, the Queen Mary and both the Queen Elizabeth ships must rank as its most famous ships.

Well-constructed solutions to engineering challenges

Successful civil engineering contractors such as McKean & Company must possess many strengths; not only must they be skilled in all current construction techniques, they must also be versatile enough to meet each new challenges posed by the changing environment.

The McKean family first established itself in the civil engineering construction sector as McKean & Renwick, Railway and Public Works Contractors, in 1918; John McKean, the founder, had previously worked as an accountant at the Coatbridge Ironworks. Since the railways were at that time the most widely-used method of transport and the rail network was still expanding, it was clearly an area of particular interest to civil engineering contractors. Not surprising, then, McKean's early projects included work on a number of railway bridges, and indeed railway work remained a significant part of the firm's business until the 1960s. But it was also involved in different kinds of civil engineering work. Projects ranged from constructing the terraces at Firhill Football Ground for Partick Thistle Football Club in 1923, to the widening of the main Oban Road through the Pass of Brander, where carrying the new section of road over Loch Awe presented something of an engineering challenge; reinforced concrete cantilevers were used to support the new road, and McKean ingeniously transported the necessary building materials to the site by boat.

During the 1930s and 40s McKean & Co's involvement in major road construction projects continued with a number of schemes in Argyll, while they also undertook various harbour and pier works, and a number of projects for the Admiralty.

One particular Admiralty project which provided McKean with an opportunity to develop a new area of expertise was the contract to build the first deep-water jetty for oil tankers

Above: *Early Bridge Works, Glasgow.*
Below: *Pinkston Cooling Tower.*

at Finnart, Loch Long (some 40 miles away from Glasgow), a project which was completed soon after the end of the war. Another unusual job was the reconstruction of the Union Canal bridge at Slateford, Edinburgh, in 1936/7. The old canal bridge, made of stone, was to be replaced by a reinforced concrete structure in order to accommodate the widening of Lanark Road. The job was complicated by the necessity of maintaining the vital water supply to Edinburgh's breweries throughout the works; in order to accomplish this it was necessary to divert the waters through pipes after damming the canal.

In the post-war period, major projects carried out by the company included the reconstruction of the cooling tower at Pinkston Power Station, Port Dundas, Glasgow, as part of the modernisation programme implemented in the mid-1950s; the total cost of the project was £263,000, and the new cooling tower was the largest one in Scotland. At around the same time the Water Department of the Corporation of the City of Glasgow was engaged on another project of great local importance; this was the completion of the final stages of a long-term programme, begun some hundred years earlier, to provide the city with drinking water from Loch Katrine. McKean was appointed to carry out the laying of additional syphon pipes across the Endrick valley in order to improve the flow of water from the Loch to the reservoirs at Milngavie.

Nineteen fifty-nine brought McKean a £18,000 contract to construct the railway trackway for the huge dock cranes at Cartsburn Dockyard, and the company subsequently explored a new dimension of railway work when it became involved with British Rail's electrification programme, carrying out work on the Glasgow/Gourock/Wemyss Bay lines. Another new venture for McKean was its involvement in one of Scotland's major developments during the 1960s - the building of Britain's first nuclear refuelling depot at Rosyth; McKean's was responsible for many of the structures at this site, with perhaps one of the most impressive examples being the huge stainless steel tank.

The following decade saw the road network growing in importance, and the construction of ring roads and bypasses became a growth area in the industry. McKean's carried out a succession of roadbuilding contracts, many in excess of of £30,000; one of the most memorable was the White Cart River Bridge at Paisley, which was constructed over a nine-month period in 1972. This impressive structure, designed by Messrs W A Fairhurst & Partners to carry the south-west leg of the Paisley Inner Ring Road over the River White Cart near Paisley Abbey, has within it 15 kilometres (nine and a half miles) of pre-stressed, post tensioned tendons.

Top: Finnart, Loch Long.

The bridge consists of twin, single-span arches with a clear span of 185 feet, with a 50' suspended deck section supported between concrete cantilevers with a span of 67' 6" each. A segmental method of construction was used, and work on the abutments had to be carried out within steel sheet pile cofferdams as the underside of the foundations lay some 8' below normal river level; so, again, this project presented McKean with some challenging aspects.

The company notched up yet another 'first' during the 1980s at the City Council's landfill site at Summerston, where it installed HDPE liner and constructed Glasgow's first leachate treatment works; and it followed this up in the 1990s by the designed and constructed building works for Scotland's first landfill gas power station, for Shanks & McEwan.

In addition to expanding its interests into environmental construction and leachate treatment, the company has in recent years become increasingly involved in design and build. With its tremendous breadth of knowledge and experience of construction projects of all types, McKean is well placed to help clients assess exactly what is involved in a particular project, in order to set realistic budgets and deadlines. Recently-completed design and build projects include Thornton Waste Transfer Station for Kirkcaldy District Council, and a new aquarium facility for Aberdeen University. While the company's involvement in design and build has become an important aspect of its current capabilities, the company sees this as complementary to its established traditions of general civil engineering construction, and bridgeworks, road works, environmental improvements and sewerage works continue to feature high on its project list.

Today, the company provides employment for around 40 local people, and for some families working for McKean has become a third-generation family tradition. Managing director Richard McKean is himself the grandson of the founder, and is determined to see the family tradition of quality and diversity carried into the next century.

Top: White Cart Bridge, Paisley.
Above left: Cartsburn Dockyard.

Glasgow College of Nautical Studies

One hundred and fifty years of nautical and marine engineering education and training in Glasgow

The Merchant Shipping Acts of 1850 and 1854 brought about the need for those who aspired to become mates and masters of merchant ships to undertake formal written and oral examinations for Certificates of Competency. Consequently a number of privately operated schools came into being, each staffed by one or two qualified master mariners, men who were the authors of the text books used by their students. Some of these publications still exist in name although they have been heavily revised and updated on numerous occasions. The Glasgow schools had riverside addresses such as Clyde Place, Robertson Street, and Oswald Street at a time when the streets on both sides of the river were occupied by all sorts of ship-related businesses - ship chandlers, paint and oil merchants, flag makers, ship furnishers, sailmakers, compass and binnacle manufacturers, compass adjusters, marine opticians and many others.

ADVERTISEMENTS.   (Brown & Son's

Nautical Academy,
41 ROBERTSON STREET,
GLASGOW.

UNDER THE PATRONAGE OF THE NOBILITY.

Conducted by CAPT. ROBB, Extra Master, and THOMAS ROBB. Passed First-Class in Nautical Astronomy under Science and Art Department, and Prizeman in Mathematics at the Glasgow West of Scotland Technical College.

OLDEST ESTABLISHED PRACTICAL SCHOOL IN GLASGOW, and the only School having *Two Teachers.* Candidates carefully and expeditiously prepared for Marine Board Examinations. Extra Masters thoroughly taught the *Mathematical Investigations of the Problems.*

COMPASS DEVIATION.

Masters, while learning the *Deviascope,* have the undivided attention of one of the Teachers. This great aid to a clear and rapid understanding of the subject of Compass Adjustment cannot be obtained at a School where there is but one Instructor. WEDNESDAY and SATURDAY FORENOONS entirely devoted to *Signals, Rule of the Road,* and *Seamanship.* Article 17 embodied in verse by Capt. Robb. This simplification of the Rule of the Road, which should be in the hands of all Seamen, can only be had at this Academy.

In 1909 the Governors of the Glasgow City Educational Endowments Board proposed the establishment of a School of Navigation in the Glasgow and West of Scotland Technical College (previously Anderson's Institute) in George Street, which was to become the Royal Technical College (in 1912), later the Royal College of Science and Technology (1956) and now the University of Strathclyde (since 1964). The idea was supported by the local shipowners including Sir

Left: *An advertisement in Brown's Nautical Almanac of 1898 for one of the private schools of navigation. At least two such schools survived until the 1920s. The language is indicative of the intense rivalry for business.* **Below:** *Captain Charles Brown (left) with students, in about 1911 when commercial sailing vessels were still afloat in relatively large numbers and caused 'Rule of the Road' problems, especially at night.*

Charles Cayzer (Clan Line), Sir Nathaniel Dunlop (Queen Line), W H Raeburn (Monarch Steamship Co), J P Macloy (Macloy and McIntyre) and Henderson Bros (Anchor Line).

The committee, constituted in January 1910 to appoint a Superintendent and oversee the operation of the School, included representatives of the College Governors, the Educational Endowment Board and the several Glasgow or Clyde Shipowners Associations including some who were predominantly sailing ship owners (eg Charles Barnie, Wm Law, Thomas Hardie). There were around a hundred Clyde-based shipping companies and agents at that time although many were "one-ship" or small companies or operated very small vessels. The appointee of the Mercantile Marine Service Association was Captain John C Black, a superintendent with Raeburn and qualified as both a Master Mariner and as a First Class Engineer. He had campaigned personally for such a school for several years and remained a member until his death in 1934.

The advertisement for the post of superintendent attracted 55 applications from which Captain Charles H Brown was appointed at a salary of £300 per annum. He had 14 years sea experience from apprentice to Master, in sail and steam, had nine years teaching experience in Dundee, and was to prove an outstanding choice. The cost of books, charts and apparatus amounted to £330, and the School opened on 27th September 1910. Captain Alex Macdonald was appointed as assistant and the Admiralty appointed a CPO Yeoman of Signals as an instructor for Morse, semaphore and the use of code flags, an arrangement which was to continue for over 50 years. In addition to day classes for mainstream students (apprentices to Extra Master) there were evening classes for yachtsmen (116 in the first year) and astronomy lectures. Day school teachers could obtain a certificate recognised

Top: Captain Alex Macdonald discussing the rigging of a full rigged ship with a student at a time when sailing vessel certificates were still sought by suitably experienced candidates; such certificates were valid for steamships. **Above:** *Photocopy of advert for MacGibbon's School of Engineering dated 1947.*

by the Scottish Education Department as a qualification to teach navigation in secondary schools.

In 1913, when wireless telegraphy on board ship was something of a novelty, the Marconi Company provided equipment for a course on the theory, construction and use of WT apparatus. Long weather reports transmitted from the Eiffel Tower were read daily. A Miss M Turnbull was the first girl to qualify as a marine wireless operator.

In terms of student hours attended annually, the School of Navigation was for many years one of the largest departments in the College. Of the 121 days students who enrolled in session 1911 - 1912, 96 were employed by 34 Glasgow shipping companies. The course for apprentices set up in 1920 became the model for colleges elsewhere and a correspondence course for apprentices was established in 1926. Having been a prime-mover in forming the Association of Navigation Schools (UK wide) of which he was the first Secretary and as the author and reviser of several standard textbooks, Captain Brown's influence on nautical education extended far beyond Glasgow until his retirement in 1939.

Marine engineering, unlike navigation and seamanship, has long had a presence in university education because of its relevance to professional employment ashore. Candidates for Certificates of Competency were catered for by private schools such as MacGibbon's, housed in Bridge Street, which lasted until the 1960s, the final Principal, James Holburn, became a member of the first College Council of the present College of Nautical Studies.

Marine engineering was, however, taught in Kent Road School until 1943 when it became a subject within the Department of Mechanical Engineering at Stow College of Engineering, largely as a result of a request from the Ministry of War Transport that better education be provided to help combat the shortage of qualified seagoing engineers. A separate Department of Marine Engineering was established in that College in 1952.

When College-based engineer cadet training with an increased academic emphasis became an alternative to the traditional engine-shop apprenticeship, an allied

Below: *Rowing practice for youngsters on a pre-sea cadet course, sometime between the two World Wars, off the north bank of the Clyde a short distance upriver from the present College. Boatwork subsequently took place at Bardowie Loch, off Ardrossan and at Blairvaddach (Rhu) but is now, once again, practised in the river.*

Department of Power Plant was set up in Springburn College (now North Glasgow College) to provide the necessary practical experience.

The WT classes offered in the early days of the Royal Technical College were disbanded with the appearance of private schools and the growth of a WT section within the Watt Memorial College (now James Watt College) in Greenock where annual enrolments grew continuously from 11 in 1918-19 to over 100 post World War II.

Above: *Apprentices practising sextant observations on the roof of the Royal Technical College, now the University of Strathclyde, in George Street, in brand-new uniforms at the conclusion of their one year course 1946-47.*

The last of the private schools, the Glasgow Wireless College (which incorporated the Scottish Signal School) closed its doors in Newton Place in the 1960s.

The present College of Nautical Studies was built in 1967/8 and the first Principal was Robert Marshall, a Marine Engineer, appointed from Stow College. The purpose was to concentrate the education and training of Merchant Navy personnel in Strathclyde on one site. The School of Navigation at the Royal College of Science and Technology (now Strathclyde University), the Marine Engineering Department of Stow College of Engineering and the Communications Department of the Watt Memorial College, Greenock, were transferred to form the nucleus of the College.

The General Studies Department was added in 1972 and in 1973 the Power Plant Practice Department of Springburn College of Engineering was transferred. The College was further expanded in 1974 by the addition of a Hall of Residence. At the beginning of 1978 Bob Marshall retired and Captain Tom Ireland, Extra Master Mariner was appointed Principal. He was previously Principal of Fleetwood Nautical College. In 1984 a Department of Mathematics and Computing was formed and in the same year the Power Plant Department and the Marine

Engineering Department combined and the structure of five College Departments continued for ten years.

In 1987 Tom Ireland retired and for the next four years Alex (Sandy) Smith, Extra 1st Class Marine Engineer, who joined the College from Stow College in 1968, served as Principal. In 1991 Captain Chris Hunter, formerly Principal of the National Sea Training College, was appointed.

In the Autumn of 1994 reorganisation was undertaken to reflect the changing education service provided by the College. The five Departments were replaced by the three Faculties, of Engineering, Science and Technology and Maritime Studies respectively and thirteen Schools were structured to assume authority for identified and distinct areas of College activity within these Faculties.

Three years later, in 1997, continued College growth necessitated the formulation of a fourth Faculty for Care and Social Studies.

Below: *The present modern College complex, situated close to the city centre on the south bank of the River Clyde, was formally opened on 4 October 1969 by Admiral of the Fleet, the Earl Mountbatten of Burma.*

The early eighties saw a decline in the recruitment for the British Merchant Navy and a rationalisation of nautical Colleges in the UK took place. In February 1985, the Secretary of State for Scotland announced his decision to centralise the provision of nautical education in Scotland at the Glasgow College of Nautical Studies. Today the College remains the sole provider of main-stream nautical education in Scotland. It provides the complete range of courses in both the navigation and engineering disciplines and is one of only three such Colleges in the United Kingdom.

The next chapter in the story of the College's development commenced in April 1993, when it was incorporated under the Further and Higher Education (Scotland) Act. The College is now funded directly by the Scottish Office Education and Industry Department. 250 young cadet officers of both deck and engineering disciplines now enter the College each August/September and for most of them so begins a long association with the College. Many of them on completing their cadetships will return, enrolling on courses for Maritime and Coastguard Agency senior certificates of competency leading to command or chief engineer rank and subsequent careers at sea or in the shore-based Shipping and related Industries.

Top: On Monday 2 November 1998, Glenda Jackson CBE MP, Minister for Shipping performed the official opening ceremony of the College's full-mission ship manoeuvring simulator. The simulator which also incorporates a state-of-the-art electronic navigation systems laboratory was installed in January 1998 and became operational in April. It is one of the most technically advanced simulators in the world and it is fitting that it should come to Glasgow, the largest ship management centre in Western Europe.

Above left: *On Thursday 26th March 1997 at an inaugural Salute to Youth and Training in the Painted Hall of the Royal Naval College, Greenwich, Glasgow College of Nautical Studies won a prestigious award for its outstanding and consistent contribution to training within the Maritime Industry. The Award was presented by European Transport Commissioner Neil Kinnock and P&O Chairman, Lord Sterling of Plaidstow, CBE at a dinner attended by 350 Industry representatives. Chris Hunter, Principal of the College, on receiving the award from Neil Kinnock, thanked those Shipping Companies who had supported the College over the years.*

Accommodating the needs of the city for almost 150 years

Glasgow in 1727 was described by Daniel Defoe as 'one of the cleanest, most beautiful and best-built cities in Great Britain.' The city's population at that time stood at somewhere around 12,500; by the end of the 18th century it had risen to over 62,000, and by the middle of the 19th century - the time when the property business which we know today as Ross and Liddell was first established - it had reached in excess of 395,000 and was still rising fast.

The reasons for this tremendous influx of people into Glasgow lay, of course, in the growth of industry and commerce in the city. The beginning of the industrial revolution at the end of the 18th century had changed the economic pattern, drawing craftsfolk away from the countryside where they had traditionally used their skills to support an independent, self-suffi-cient lifestyle, and concentrating the workforce in towns and cities all over Great Britain. Many workers settled in the new Glasgow suburbs of Tradeston, Hutchesontown and Laurieston around this time. The opening of the Forth and Clyde Canal to Port Dundas in 1790 also brought in new trade, and communities grew up at the Calton and Anderston where the new cotton mills provided mass employment. Increasingly, the cottage industries found that they could not compete with the mills and factories in the towns, and the country folk had little choice but to leave the impoverished country areas where they had grown up and go in search of employment. A significant number of Irish immigrants were also coming to Scotland, believing that the new industries there would bring them prosperity. So Glasgow was crowded with thousands of people who had come looking for

*Above: An example of the company's present day advertising. **Below:** Traditional blocks of quality tenement property.*

in premises at 24 Rutherglen Road in 1854, would have had no shortage of clients amongst the shifting population of Glasgow in the mid-19th century. As the new working-class moved in, the former occupants of these areas moved out, leaving the now overcrowded city centre in favour of superior housing in the suburbs. Overcrowding remained a problem, however, and it was clear that more housing was needed to accommodate the city's workforce. Already, in the first half of the 19th century, some very fine tenement housing had been erected in Laurieston, and the 1860s saw the beginning of the development of a series of large new working-class suburbs; Bridgeton, Dalmarnock, Springburn, Partick, Govan, Govanhill and Maryhill all date back to this time. Alexander Barron's property management business was prospering; it had moved to 5 Alston Street in 1859, then to 94 South Portland Street two years later, and in 1865, trading as A and R Barron, it was able to move into the very heart of the commercial centre, taking offices first at 128 Union Street and the following year, at 5 Dixon Street. As the building boom continued the firm expanded steadily, and in 1876 the prosperous business changed its name to T Ross.

Meanwhile, eight miles away in Paisley another housing

work; the new immigrant communities established themselves in the city centre, as is usually the case, taking over the old properties in the High Street, Gallowgate, Saltmarket and Bridegate.

This movement led to a buoyant property market, and Mr Alexander Barron, who had set up shop as a house factor

Above: A good example of the quality of decorative tilework seen in many Glasgow closes and staircases.
Top: An example of a residential development showing the changing face of Glasgow's industrial heritage.

factor was having a rather more difficult time. Formed in 1828 by Mr Andrew Deans and carried on after his death 11 years later by Mr James Winning, this firm had struggled through a great trade recession which had hit Paisley's spinning industry so hard that almost a third of the workforce had no regular income. In 1839 James Winning's firm became Winning and Gordon after being taken over by Mr Gordon, who retired in 1848; a lifelong supporter of the temperance movement, Mr Gordon was commemorated after his death by a monument erected by his friends in that movement. He left no family heir to the business, however, and in due course Mr William Fulton joined the business which in 1886 adopted the name of

Winning and Fulton. By this time the thriving shipbuilding industry had restored economic prosperity to Paisley, with shipbuilders John Fullarton and Company building some 60 vessels of up to 500 tons between 1867 and 1883 and generating work for many smaller firms in the district.

In 1888 the collapse of the City of Glasgow Bank, upon which much of the local building industry depended for its finance, brought building activity in Glasgow to a

Above: *A typical sandstone block of traditional offices and shops.*

sudden halt and put a number of building firms out of business, but by the early 1890s other firms had taken their place and the construction of new housing had resumed its momentum. By this time, too, much had been learned about the importance of good planning, and a wider understanding of the links between poor sanitation and disease had given rise to increased hygiene-consciousness. This new social awareness was reflected in the housing which was built during this period, which was of a higher standard than previously; often, too, the fronts of tenements featured oriel or bow windows. Glasgow was once again living up to Defoe's praise a century and a half earlier. Property management companies such as T Ross, which in 1898 changed its name to Ross and Liddell, were able to offer prospective tenants accommodation which was of a very high standard indeed. The stylistic attraction of the buildings being erected was further enhanced, in many people's opinion, by the new architectural trend which began during the last decade of the 19th century of bringing in pink freestone from

Ayrshire and Dumfriesshire for use on frontages, instead of the local white stone. The pink stone was widely used in the construction of properties at Hyndland, Battlefield and other suburbs built at that time, although the best example of its use is probably Charing Cross Mansions, a massive block in the French Renaissance style.

The vogue for elaborate architecture continued throughout the late Victorian and Edwardian era. The many substantial tenement blocks which were built during this period were both spacious and aesthetically pleasing, but the economic pattern was by now poised ready to make another shift, this time away from Glasgow. Although the city continued to be regarded as one of the greatest shipbuilders in the world, other industries disappeared, and Glasgow's period of great prosperity and optimism was at an end. The infamous Rent Act passed by Lloyd George's government also had a major impact on the pattern of housing, discouraging the speculative builder by limiting the profit potential, and placing the onus of providing housing upon the local authority.

Glasgow responded first with Mosspark and similar small garden suburbs, then, extending the city boundaries in 1912, with larger developments such as Pollok and Knightswood, before the building programme was disrupted by the outbreak of World War I. When peace returned, provision of housing was a priority, and, encouraged by Government incentives, the city embarked on huge estates like Castlemilk, Drumchapel and Easterhouse. As more and more workers were accommodated in council housing, property management agents found that much of their business had been effectively taken away from them. Small firms stood little chance of surviving, and Ross and Liddell began to pursue a policy of expansion through acquisition, beginning with the takeover of the property firm of Mackinnon and Browning in 1949, and going on to acquire James G Lynn in 1965 and Alexander Sinclair in 1973; in 1974 it acquired Robert Stobo and Bathgate, R D Paton and Thomas Stobbs and Sons, followed by James Patterson and Co in 1975 and James McMeekin in 1977, and in 1979, the year that it became a limited company, it acquired Thomas McGill.

In Paisley in the aftermath of the Rent Act Winning and Fulton had had to face similar problems; having been appointed as the Town's first burgh factor to manage the first municipal houses when they were built in 1922, this service was later taken over by the council's own factors, and Winning and Fulton transferred its attentions instead to the insurance and property valuation markets. The company had been for a long time an agent for the Phoenix Assurance Company Ltd, and was responsible for placing policies for top Paisley industrialists such as J and P Coats and J and J Clark. In 1971 Winning & Fulton, too, embarked on the expansion route taking over the Paisley firm of WL Kirkwood.

Meanwhile Glasgow was continuing to spread, and after a further extension to the city boundaries in 1938, concern

Above: *Charing Cross Mansions at the turn of the century.*

high, as happened at Red Road in 1962, thousands of people could be accommodated in brand new homes of their own. It did not work, of course; even people who desperately wanted their own home found it difficult to accept the need to live in isolation miles off the ground and cut off from central amenities, any more than they found it acceptable to live many miles out of town and spend several hours of every day commuting to work and back. Like any workforce, what most of them wanted was simply somewhere that was spacious enough to raise a family in comfort, close enough to their workplace and to the amenities to be convenient, and modest enough to be affordable. The existing Victorian and Edwardian tenement blocks, which had fallen into neglect while other housing schemes were tried out, met all these criteria, and property management companies were once again able to meet the housing needs of Glasgow's workers by supervising the refurbishment of many of the city centre's tenements.

began to grow over the fact that the occupants of the new estates were many miles away from the city centre where many of them worked, as well as the amount of surrounding countryside which was being eaten up by these schemes. This led to the notion of building upwards rather than outwards. Many readers will remember the introduction of the concept of multi-storey flats in the 1950s, when the idea was hailed as the answer towards the city's housing problems. By building blocks of flats ten storeys high, hundreds of people could be provided with living space; and by building blocks of flats 31 storeys

Ross and Liddell today maintain all types of residential properties - single tenement buildings, housing estates both small and large, or multi-storey developments with

Above left: *A modern commercial development of shops and offices.*

In addition to property management and maintenance, Ross and Liddell provide a comprehensive range of residential and commercial services, including estate agency, surveys, valuations, insurance, investment and marketing advice, rent reviews, development appraisals, compulsory purchase negotiations, rating appeals and council tax appeals. As letting agents they undertake rent collection, tenant vetting, rent roll maintenance, and provide advice to tenants on leases, furnishings, rental values and legal requirements. In dealing with the varied housing needs of the Glasgow of today, the firm is able to call upon not far short of a century and a half's experience of meeting the needs of a constantly moving workforce, and whether it is helping tenants find the right type of accommodation for themselves or letting property on behalf of Glaswegians who are temporarily relocating elsewhere, Ross and Liddell knows the importance of providing a swift, efficient, sympathetic and professional service.

Ross and Liddell's progressive business strategy includes sophisticated management techniques and a high level of computerisation which is designed to maximise efficiency, and its enthusiastic team, backed by senior personnel with many years experience in the business of property management and surveying, is ready to meet the challenges of the new millennium. One of Scotland's oldest property management companies, Ross and Liddell has an important role to play in the future development of the city, where new ideas will interact with the best of the past to create the Glasgow of the future.

leisure facilities. They are committed to urban renewal, handling tenement developments, refurbishments and major repair schemes involving projects in excess of £1 million. A specialised department of building surveyors was set up in the early 1980s to deal principally with tenement refurbishment, and this service today has expanded to offer, in addition, a wide range of services in connection with the alteration and repair of buildings, such as structural surveys, Schedules of Dilapidations, and modernisation, repair and alteration of properties.

Early in 1988 Ross and Liddell amalgamated with Winning and Fulton, with each company initially retaining its own trading name and its own premises. Ross and Liddell continues to operate from its offices at 60 Enoch Square, which it has occupied since 1972, and also from 25 Gauze Street, Paisley. Working in partnership rather than in competition has brought many benefits to both companies, with a broader client base, wider influence and greater freedom to pursue new business over a wider area. This joint venture, which in 1994 incorporated William Goudie & Son of Paisley, decided to create a unified image and now trades solely under the name of Ross & Liddell, bringing them to the forefront of property management in the West of Scotland.

Above left: *A fine example of an out of town development.* ***Above:*** *A warehouse converted to residential flats under further refurbishment.*

Tradition and technology

Steeped in more than 150 years of craftsmanship and traditon, Glasgow-based upholstery leather specialist Andrew Muirhead & Son Limited is today at the very forefront of technology.

Recognised world-wide as a producer of high performance, quality leather, Andrew Muirhead, based in Bridgeton, produces more than 2,500 hides a week for both the UK and over 45 countries world-wide. It is global leader in the aviation leather market, producing flame retardant leather for over 15 airlines, airframe and seating manufacturers in more than 30 countries around the world. It is estimated that, globally, at least 15 million passengers sat on Andrew Muirhead leather covered seats last year!

The company also produces leather for furniture upholstery (both domestic and corporate) and

Right: *Late payers are not new! A customers Statement back in 1893.*
Below: *Inspection and Measuring hides circa 1922.*

specialist car markets. It has a skilled workforce of more than 100 local men and women, many of whom have been with the company all their working lives.

Although nowadays much of the work is automated and computerised. tanning and finishing is still labour intensive. The wet blue hides (leather which has been tanned, but not further processed) are taken

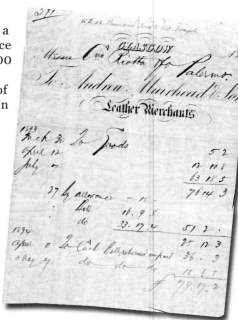

This picture: *A production order for HM Government circa 1912.*

through the finishing process to produce a range of beautiful leathers in hundreds of colours - colour coated full grain leathers, calf soft semi-anilines and super soft aniline leathers.

The company also carries out many custom contracts where a particular type, colour or matching is required.

The Muirhead association with leather can be traced back to 1758 when they first owned a tannery near Glasgow, although it was not until 1840 that Andrew Muirhead first named his business. In 1870 the business moved to its present site in Dunn Street and after a period specialising in a variety of leather types, the company shifted its emphasis in the 60s to high performance upholstery leathers.

Above: *A fire in 1944 destroyed a significant part of the Dunn Street facility revealing the tenement buildings opposite.*

Small businesses as well as large multi-national corporations call on the services of Andrew Muirhead, particularly where there are specialist requirements. For example recently the company produced a small piece of gold leaf-stamped leather for a book cover, leather chairs with a printed pattern for a restaurant and even matched some leather to the colour of a pecan nut (sent through the post) for another customer.

Committed to ongoing technical and service-based development Andrew Muirhead has its own in-house technical team who constantly strive to develop new generation leather. A recent coup was the creation of the industry's first dedicated Civil Aviation Authority approved in-house fire testing facility offering leading-edge flame retardant leather.

Andrew Muirhead is proud of its Glasgow traditions and glad to play its part in the success of the city, especially through its position as a world leader in the supply of upholstery leather to the Aerospace Industry. It has recently acquired the nght to use the Scotland the Brand logo on all its literature.

Recognition of the company's profession-alism, customer service and care of its workforce has been given by both industry and the government with the registration of BS/ISO 9002 in 1988 and a BSI Kitemark licence in 1989. Both achievements were the first of their kind in the industry world-wide.

Above: A woodcarving of the factory circa 1880.
Below: Modern day 'Shaving' of upholstery hides.

The firm that 'takes the biscuit'

To most people, Tunnock's means Caramel Wafers, and to people fortunate enough to live near their Bakery and Tea-room it also means the aroma of freshly-baked bread. It was Thomas Tunnock, son of a stonemason, who began the family tradition of baking and established the firm of Thomas Tunnock in 1890.

Tom went from school to serve his apprenticeship in Aberdour Bakery, on Old Mill Road.
By dint of working and saving, at the age of 25 he was able to buy a small shop and bakery, with contents, at Lorne Place in Bellshill Road. He provided food and service for celebrations and special occasions; a report in the Hamilton Herald and Lanarkshire Weekly News dated December 1890 makes reference to "an excellent tea, provided by Bro. Thomas Tunnock" at the annual social meeting of The Loyal Order of Ancient Shepherds, an insurance society of which Tom Tunnock was a member - and which still exists today as The Shepherds Friendly Society. Tom had a strong interest in local matters, and he began a tradition of helping local causes which subsequent generations have carried on in spectacular fashion.

Picnics and excursions in Edwardian times were fairly formal occasions, and Tom was often called

upon to supply a good selection of fresh baked savouries and sweet things for everybody. He also provided the food at the League of the True Cross's socials and the Gospel Band's tea-meetings. Besides advertising his willingness to cater for any event from a Bridal Banquet to a Celebration High Tea, Tom was always full of novel ideas to increase trade and bring new customers to the bakery. One ploy was to invite customers to bring along their own butter and let him bake it into the purest quality short-bread for them; another was having the customer's favourite local view painted onto a shortbread farl. He then hit upon the idea of opening a tea-room, which he advertised as a 'COMMERCIAL DINING ROOM for Socials, Smokers and Presentations. Ladies' Accommodation'. This proved a success, and the dining room was well-patronised.

In 1892 Thomas married Mary Mitchell, a 21-year old dairymaid. Their son Archibald was born in 1895 and their daughter Alice in 1903. By 1906 Archibald was one of six boys employed by his

Above: Thomas and Mary Tunnock with a young Archibald. Below: Thomas Tunnock's Shop and Tea-room on Bellshill Road, at the turn of the century.

father to go round the village selling ha'penny rolls. These they carried in large baskets, each holding 72 rolls; the villagers would leave their doors open and the boys would leave the rolls on the kitchen table, returning for the money on Saturday when the weekly wage had been paid. Sometimes when times were hard the womenfolk would only be able to pay part of what they owed, on account. At such times competition for what money there was in the village became cut-throat, and Tunnock's resorted to offering five rolls for tuppence. Trading conditions were to become even more difficult, and in the years before the first world war the bakery business could not support the whole family, so Archie bought a Ford and an Argyle and started a small car hire firm. He began to develop an enthusiasm for cars and the motor trade, but unfortunately his car-hire venture was short-lived; in 1916 he sold up, joined up, and was sent to Iraq, where he remained for three years. His father, meanwhile, struggled to maintain his trade, but ill-health forced him to close the bakery in 1919. He died the following year, at the age of only 54. His son was unaware of these sad events until he returned home a fortnight after Tom's death. Archie had not been intending to return to the trade, but he had a change of heart and he and his mother re-opened the now-derelict bakery. With Mrs Tunnock 'holding on to the till', Archie baked, beginning with simple items such as morning rolls, small Paris buns and doughnuts. He was later able to re-employ one of his father's bakers, Michael Scott, who stayed with the firm for the remainder of his working life.

During the early 1920's, when the miners' strikes were causing a great deal of hardship, Archie was responsible for providing school meals at several local schools, which, as the children were given three meals a day, amounted to a considerable volume of work. In 1924 Archie was able to open a new, larger Bakers and Tea-room in the Main Street, which is still there today, and still has its original shopfront.

Archie followed his father's tradition of catering for local functions, and among his most popular feasts were 'Steak Pie Teas', Burns' Suppers and food for Christmas and New Year parties. He took care to give his customers the same personal attention for which his father had been famous, and it was this personal service which kept Tunnock's ahead of the fierce competition from other bakers in the area. Of an evening, Archie Tunnock would drop in on every single function at which they were purveying to make sure that all was running smoothly - and on one particular evening the firm was providing six separate 'Installation Harmony Teas' in six different Masonic Halls! Archie's 'right-hand man' at this time was Clunie Macpherson, who gave many years of loyal service to the firm. All the staff worked hard; Archie himself took no holidays and worked up to 18 hours a day. In the early days they had only three vans, which were kept busy transporting food and equipment to the various halls, bringing the china and cutlery back to be washed up during the early hours of the morning, and setting off again at six am with the morning rolls.

Top: *A rather ornate invoice from 1909.* ***Right:*** *Purveying for High Tea in 1928. Alice Tunnock is pictured left.*

Tunnock's were fortunate during the second world war in that they managed to secure generous allocations for essential items; they made trifles by the thousand and sent them by tram-car to shops all over the West of Scotland, and kept their local customers supplied with fresh buns and cakes throughout the war. In 1945 Tunnock's organised a gymkhana to welcome Uddingston's men and women home from the war; Archie had put on events of this nature before and had a flair for organisation and publicity, and it was a terrific success, attracting huge crowds and raising £2,500, which was redistributed in the form of a £5 gift to each man and woman. Archie was a generous, helpful and happy man, regarded by his employees with the greatest of affection. He was full of enthusiasm for both his work and his hobbies; he liked animals and had his own little zoo, he enjoyed cricket and sponsored Uddingston's Cricket Club, and he retained his interest in cars - although his usual mode of transport was his 'work bike', he owned a Rover 3-litre and a Rolls Royce.

Real prosperity came after the end of the second world war, when business picked up and there was a seemingly insatiable demand for sweet things. A larger bakery, the New Daylight Bakery, was built; opened in 1947 and incorporating many labour-saving devices, it was extended in 1962 and again in 1965. Biscuits continued to sell, but what Archie really wanted for the firm was a speciality item; he experimented with dry wafers and caramel and finally created the Caramel Wafer. Introduced in 1951 and baked to a secret recipe which defies imitation, this has become the firm's best-seller. It was exported under the name of 'Piper' Caramel Wafers, with a picture of a Scots bagpipe player on the wrapper. During the 50s, following the success of Caramel Wafers, Tunnock's introduced Snowballs (soft mallow covered with chocolate and

Top: *David Spiers and Archie Tunnock (right) pictured in the bakery in 1920.*
Left: *Producing the shells for Mutton Pies in 1934.*

coconut), Caramel Logs, Tea Cakes and Wafer Creams. During the 60s the company began producing its own chocolate, made in vats from the purest cocoa butter, cane sugar and full cream chocolate crumb.

Today the factory bakes a full range of traditional Scottish products for their shop in Uddingston. Besides chocolate, which is stored in large tanks and used to cover and fill several different kinds of biscuits, 15 tons of caramel are produced each day and spread onto wafers (these days, by machine) to produce some four million of the famous Caramel Wafers each week. And the firm's fleet of vans has grown all bright red and bearing the driver's name on the back - a well-known trade mark in Glasgow and the West of Scotland. The importance of presentation and packaging, along with the catchy adver-tising slogans which Thomas and his son Archie after him used to love coining, has always been recognised by the firm; it was Archie who discovered that by using gaily-coloured display boxes, which cost one penny more than plain cardboard, he could almost double his sales of mallows and wafers.

Archie's two sons Thomas and Boyd were both active in the family business for many years; Tom was responsible for overseeing the launching of the Caramel Wafer and contributed enormously to the success of the firm until his untimely death in 1992. His brother Boyd is Chairman and Managing Director, with daughters, Karen and

Fiona, actively involved in the firm as Directors, upholding the firm's maxim of Quality and Value as he steers the successful family business into the new millennium.

Above: Batter mix being poured in the wafer ovens in the late 1950s.
Below: Boyd Tunnock crossing off the old employment figure and adding the newest one to one of their delivery vans in the 1980s.

Painting a bright future for Scotland

James Hastings Lightbody MC will still be remembered by many people as an exceptional individual with many outstanding qualities. After a distinguished military career, during which he worked his way up through the ranks to become a Captain and won the Military Cross at Gallipoli, he sold Rolls Royce motor cars on behalf of Clyde Automobile Company for a while, before setting up his own business in 1936.

From the very start, Lightbody's was run as a family business. The founder's wife, a well-known and popular figure in the motor trade throughout the region, was actively involved in the business during its formative years and indeed throughout her life, taking on everything from book-keeping and credit control to serving on the committees of various motor trade organisations. Annie, as she was known, was a real character, well-respected by her fellow committee members and leading industry figures. Annie was a shrewd business-woman in her own right even before Lightbody's was set up. she worked closely with the M.D of Castlebank Laundries in the 1920s and reputedly wrote most of their advertising slogans. Her drive and determination were essential factors in the early success of the company. Annie was the daughter of a coachman and was brought up in a mews cottage in Ashton Lane which is now a smart west end restaurant. The story is told of how Annie's father used to keep an old retired mare which used to kick the stable door at 3.30pm to be let out. Her father would open the latch and the horse would walk down the Byres road on its own to wait outside the school for Annie to ride slowly home.

James and Annie's son, James Alexander, started working part-time at his father's new business when he was only 13. He was a quick learner, and it soon became apparent that he had the makings of a gifted salesman. In fact he was destined to spend most of his working life out on the road, travelling round to meet the new customers that would make the firm grow; and this remained an aspect of his work which he enjoyed enormously.

Lightbody's first took part in the Scottish Motor Show in 1949 and thereafter became a regular participant, setting an annual tradition which continued unbroken for many decades. Members of the Lightbody family also played an active part in organising a number of successful Scottish Motor Shows during the 1950s and '60s, and their involvement in this high-profile event helped bring them to prominence, as members of the Scottish Motor Trade Association and as influential figures in the regional motoring community.

In the early days the main activity of the firm was to supply coach-building accessories, such as paint and consumable materials, for new motor vehicle bodies and vehicles under repair. The business developed as the popularity of motoring grew, and Lightbody's saw the opportunity to supply 'car furnishings' - all the components which were often not supplied with new cars at the time, such as wing mirrors, heaters, driving lamps - and even wipers and extra seats in some cases.

During the second world war the company played an important role in the local supply chain -albeit with some modifications to their product range. A carefully-preserved price list from 1942 highlights some of the items on offer at that time: blackout paint, camouflage paint, ARP Red Cross Cases, and water bottles (for drinking water) in either aluminium or enamel. Dark glasses for use with incendiary bombs were priced at 2/9 (14 pence in today's currency) a pair; blackout curtaining was also available but the customer was warned they might find 'delivery and price uncertain'.

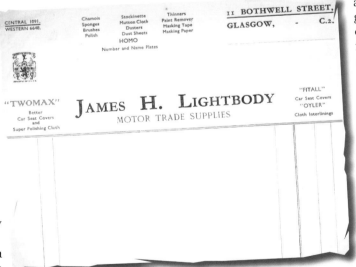

Top left: James Hastings Lightbody, founder of the company. *Above:* An early invoice. *Above right:* Annie Lightbody c1918.

The frantic official was desperate to obtain several hundred pairs of industrial gloves - to be delivered immediately to rescue workers who were digging out survivors from the hundreds of properties flattened by the bombs. The gloves were in stock, and James Lightbody set off to make one of the most vital deliveries the company would ever make. The haunting memory of his drive through the bombed-out streets, past the leaking, flame-belching gas mains, the huge craters and the pitiful casualties, would remain with James Lightbody forever. James' talents were not limited to the world of business; he was also a skilled sculptor and model-maker, and when time permitted he would fashion radiator mascots for the cars of friends in the motor trade, including one in the shape of an Afghan hound for the wife of one local dealer, and one in the shape of a Standard Poodle for the wife of another.

Horses were always a passion of James Alexander Lightbody and he carried out many commissions for trophies on this theme despite being completely untutored. Such was his skill that he exhibited in the Royal Scottish Academy for many years. One summer, in between customer calls, he took his portfolio to the Glasgow School of Art and was pleased to report their reaction: "If its not horses, I've a lot to learn. If it's horses, I can teach them."

Captain Lightbody volunteered for war service and soon found himself running a Prisoner of War camp on the Isle of Man, looking after hundreds of Italian prisoners and latterly high-ranking Nazis. Running a business of this type was classed as a reserved occupation and son James Alexander eagerly took the task on, in addition to manning an anti-aircraft battery on the outskirts of the city at night. Just one example of the impact which the war had on daily life is the story of how James Lightbody was woken by a call from a local ARP official in the early hours of the morning after Clydebank had suffered a particularly heavy bombing raid.

Above: *The North Street premises in the 1960s.*
Top: *The Lightbody stand at the 1955 Scottish Motor Exhibition.*

The late 1950s and 1960s were boom times in the motor accessory market. Local garages sold vast quantities of car-relating products to the motoring public, such as de-icer, car polish and oil additives, all of which had been sold wholesale to them by Lightbody's; this was long before supermarkets and DIY stores became involved in the motor accessory distribution chain. However, as time went on and the accessory market changed, it became clear that Lightbody would have to find new markets if the business was to grow and develop. In 1969 an association with Berger was formed, which would mark the start of the firm's concen-

tration on the supply of car finishes for specialist applications in the automotive trade. In the days of hand-made traditional black-and-white number plates, one of Lightbody's boasts was that they supplied the plates for more Scottish vehicles than any other firm. In more recent times the business' change of direction has made them one of the biggest suppliers of paints and coatings for all types of automotive and industrial applications. Besides the paints themselves, they supply bodyshop equipment such as sprayguns, compressors and crash repair equipment, acting as distributors for the leading specialist manufacturers in this field. Bodyshops throughout Scotland rely on Lightbody's for all their equipment as well as their consumables stocks which might include abrasive sealers, Health and Safety items products and sundry items such as valeting and janitorial products. Expert technical assistance is also available to existing and future customers alike; a colourist, supported by a full technical department, is usually able to help with paint and colour-related problems within 24 hours of being contacted.

His services are often called upon by customers outside the automotive industry, for example by architects and sign manufacturers who need to co-ordinate and match particular shades of colour. The company's approach to supplying paints and equipment is based on understanding the customers' needs and responding to them, and this one of the principles that has typified JH Lightbody in all its dealings. The good relationships which have grown up

Above: JA Lightbody c1980.
Below: The North Street premises in the late 1970s. Robert Moore is second from the right.

use of equipment from the wide range available the company has a wealth of experience and technical knowledge upon which to draw. Sometimes, too, industrial processes are adapted to bodyshop applications, and here again Lightbody's first-hand knowledge of applications outside the automotive industry is of immense value.

Jim Lightbody, grandson of the founder and current managing director abandoned a career path in accountancy to join the family business. He is all in favour of progress. Modern stock control systems have been introduced to enhance speed of service. The company has all the latest technology including spectrophometry for colour identification and formulation, and customers can, if they wish, place their orders electronically. But what many customers value most of all is the high quality service provided by knowledgeable, experienced and friendly staff, and they can be sure that at Lightbody's the personal touch will never be lost.

As this book goes to print the doors are about to be closed on the North Street premises for the last time. A brand new purpose-built unit is being prepared for occupation around the start of the new millennium, and the firm is moving into temporary premises to permit a new development on the North Street site. The new premises will occupy a prime site just north of the city centre well connected to the motorway network and will incorporate state of the art technology and and distribution systems. Co-incidentally, the motor trade connection will continue in North Street as the new occupier seems likely to be Glasgow's first Harley Davidson motorcycle distributor.

between the firm and its business associates are based on trust and shared interests, and are due in no small part to the efforts of the loyal workforce. The long-serving employees who have devoted their working lives to the business are valued highly by the company, and it is especially proud that two members of staff can claim over 100 years' service between them; one of them, Robert Moore, with over 50 years service, who retired as general manager but has returned to work on a part time basis. His colleague George Brown has almost completed his half century and today still calls on customers as he did when he first started with the company.

New products, new finishes and new systems are constantly being launched onto the market; Lightbody's has seen technology develop and improve tremendously over the years, and when advising customers on the selection and

Above: *One of the 1980s fleet.*
Top: *The trade counter in the 1970s.*

'Diamond D' Shipping

Many an exciting tale has started with an office clerk running away to a life of adventure at sea. The hardships and failure which fate meted were avoided by young James Denholm, founder of the company which bears his name. As premature head of his family he started work in a law office aged fourteen, loathed it but wisely learned, and saved, all he could. By the time he was twenty in 1866 the determined youngster was established as a Factor and Land Agent in Greenock.

From this base he set out to build up a seagoing clientele among the Brixham schooners trading between London and Glasgow. By 1869, when his sixteen year old brother, John, joined him, he was registered as a Shipping Agent and Shipbroker. With phenomenal drive the brothers outstripped their rivals to establish a shipping firm which has grown under twin brotherly management for over a century.

The Denholm's first vessel was the David Sinclair, a 122 ton Brixham topsail schooner. The bank considered the young business men far too young to be taken seriously but two local men knew the Denholms better and put up the £2,500. Under the Denholms she ran coal to the West Indies and Americas and returned with grain, pine resin and sugar. Soon after, in 1875, James Denholm died of tuberculosis.

Six years later John Denholm married his first wife and by 1882 the young company had grown to twelve wooden sailing ships engaged in the West Indies trade. The change-over from sail to steam, by way of imperfect composite ships combining sail with steam engines whose coal took profit making cargo space, was by trial and error. By 1882, when Denholms purchased their first steel steamship the Carronpark, for £8,300, these problems had been resolved and the beautiful wooden sailing ships were beginning to fade into history.

For the next century, and more, of Denholm's existence all their ensuing ships bore the suffix ...park at the end of their name. As their modern fleet grew the sailing vessels was sold off to other operators. With true Scots thrift the ships' names were kept to two syllables as it was found that longer names cost more in telegraph communication charges. For example seven Denholm ships have proudly borne the name Mountpark.

***Both pictures on this page:** (Below) David Sinclair, the first ship owned by Denholms and (above) the log book for a journey made by the David Sinclair in 1874 from Brixham to Italy and on to New York. During the journey the ship was subject to storm damage and the Master, Mr Brittain was later charged with the manslaughter of the ship's cook.*

Above: John and James Denholm c1870.
Below: The launch of the SS Garvelpark in 1901. The small boy on the front row is John C Denholm, who later became chairman of the company.

Following the death of his first wife, John Denholm remarried, in 1891, another Jane who gave him seven children including the next pair of brothers, John and William, to work as a team in building the Denholm empire. She died in 1901 after which John Senior remarried her sister Jessie prior to becoming President of the Greenock Chamber of Commerce and Provost of Greenock. In 1909 management of all Denholm ships was rationalised by bringing them under the unifying flag of The Denholm Line Steamers Ltd with a share capital of £42,800 in the days when the pound sterling was worth £50 today.

All merchant ships relied on a world wide chain of coaling stations protected by the Royal Navy and the long lasting Pax Britannica to enable sea born trade to function. The sea, as always, proved as much an enemy as a friend as storms and inhospitable shores were, and are, a constant danger to seafarers including the skilled captains of The Denholm Line. In the newly renamed company's first two years four Diamond D ships were in accidents. Such events, long before the installation of radar in merchant vessels, were regarded as a part of the normal hazards of the sea and Denholms, like other ship owners, had a policy of building regular replacements.

In 1913 John Denholm, aged 59, commanded a fleet of seven ships valued at £89,000. In the first year of the Great War four of his vessels were requisitioned by HMG and the Admiralty while the Garvelpark, moored in Danzig, was seized by the Germans. Undeterred Denholms ordered three new ships equipped with electric light, a shipboard innovation at the time, at a total cost of £100,000. Two of John Denholm's younger sons saw service in the Royal Navy while a third went to sea as an apprentice.

The immediate post war years saw ships returned to the company flag, compensation paid for those lost and the newer vessels equipped with wireless operated by a fairly new breed of officer known as 'Sparks'. The new Denholm Shipping Company bought and sold ships one of which had seen war service as a Q-ship, as the disguised armed merchantmen submarine hunters were known.

From 1921 sea going trade was subject to a decade of see-saw series of depressions and fluctuations brought about by higher costs, strikes and falling freight rates. John Denholm, who became President of the UK Chamber of Shipping, steered his company successfully through these difficult years until as an octogenarian he handed the helm to his son John from 1934. Increasing trade in the later thirties saw the Denholm fleet established with nine vessels and another two on order when World War II broke out to change the world again.

As before ships were requisitioned and staff called up. Nine company vessels were sunk, the majority by torpedo attacks from submarines, and both the Greenock and London offices were bombed in air raids. John Denholm was awarded the CBE for his service with the Ministry of War Transport, while his brother William commanded 77th Highland Field Regiment at Dunkirk and beyond.

The decision to rebuild the Denholm fleet after the war was regarded, by many shipowners, as folly. As things turned out the two brothers were able to make a success of the venture by wise, even lucky, buying and cost effective chartering to rebuild their line to seven ships. They expanded into the fields of oil and ore carrying which later became dominated by the giant bulk carriers.

Pre-war independent family businesses were being replaced by consortia and mergers to provide the benefits of size which are such a feature of modern business. First Denholms allied themselves with

Above: *Lieutenant JC Denholm RNVR, on board HMS Ladybird in 1917.*
Below: *Mountpark, which was built in 1912, ran aground in the River Forth. CLoser inspection reveals a crew member being brought ashore by breeches buoy.*

other Scottish companies and then with Norwegian firms eventually managing fourteen American owned Naess ships. Following in the family tradition of adapting to circumstances the Denholms went in for ship management rather than shipowning and rapidly became one of the largest ship management concerns in the world. By the mid 1960s this fleet numbered 48 ships with a combined tonnage of 1,332,000 cwt.

Modern training, manning and management techniques to supply well qualified and adaptable officers and crews enabled Denholms to bridge the old ship-shore divide between seamen and managers. A new construction team supervised ship building projects. In the 1970s minibulkers of 3,000 tons were developed for short voyages and small loads while another Denholm enterprise organised the Atlantic Bulkers Pool of 30,000 ton bulk carriers operating as the 'tramps steamers' of yore to go where trade was. In the same decade Denholms managed the first British ships to be

powered by jet aircraft type gas turbine engines which turned the biggest variable pitch propellers then fitted to merchantmen.

Adverse trading conditions, such as the OPEC oil embargoes, made the 1970s a difficult era although Denholms were managing one percent of the world's shipping tonnage. The firm diversified its operations, initially by acquiring a travel company, to expand its onshore enterprises at a time when Asian crews were replacing more costly European seamen and national flags were giving way to flags of convenience which allowed for cheaper running costs and, in many cases, lower standards of seamanship and safety than demanded by the Board of Trade.

Denholms today are worth over £40M, less than half of which is in shipping, while 600 people, of a total workforce of 2,000, work ashore in the UK alone. The Denholm Seafoods enterprise is one of the major players in this sector of the market with some 80 fishing vessels, nine fish selling ports and four fish factories. Denholm has also diversified into Industrial Services, specialising in fabric maintenance for oil related structures offshore and for a range of industries onshore. The Agency and Forwarding division has offices in ten British ports to cater for shippers and ship owners requiring warehousing and cargo space. The Denholm Group faces the future as a more diverse and better balanced business than ever before.

Top: *The Vancouver Forest, built in 1969, under heavy ice.*
Above: *Ga Chau, the renamed Wellpark, is one of the two ships owned by Denholms today.*

The traditional blend giving true Scottish value

It was the early years of the 20th century, and Walter Kyle, a young engineer, left the shores of his native Scotland to look for gold in Africa. He pegged a likely claim, sampled some quartz, and found he had struck gold. His dreams of creating a vast fortune from the elusive metal were not to last, however; after only a few years the gold-bearing seam disappeared and Walter Kyle returned to Scotland. It was then that he joined forces with a friend and found himself involved in producing gold bars of a different kind!

His friend, William Haddow, was in the business of repackaging margarine into bars suitable for household use. The two men combined their skills and together started up a margarine manufacturing business in an abandoned munitions factory in Dennistoun - an ideal location for storage of the barrels and drums of oils involved in the process. The business took off - and Cardowan Creameries was incorporated in 1930.

The years of the second world war were difficult ones for the margarine industry, which came under the jurisdiction of the Ministry of Food; wartime rationing required them to sell traders less than they wanted to buy. Walter Kyle's nephew Andrew returned from military service in time to face

Below: The transport fleet in the 1930s.

the next challenge, which came when rationing ended in 1953.

At last housewives across Britain could tear up their ration books and Cardowan were able to sell as much margarine as they wanted - yet frustratingly they had no existing customer base to build on. Gradually, however, the 'King Cole' company logo became a familiar sight around the streets of Glasgow as the company's fleet of delivery vehicles increased.

The year 1956 brought its own setbacks when a huge fire ripped through the building. The Glasgow Fire Service battled with the blaze, but could not save the factory from serious damage. The skeleton of steel beams - an inheritance from the days when Beardmore manufactured munitions on the premises - survived, though the fire was serious enough to close the Cardowan factory down for a year.

The past 70 years have seen many changes in the margarine production process. In earlier days whale oil, delivered in wooden casks, was a key ingredient of margarine. Today the old wooden casks have given way to tanker loads of animal and vegetable oils, which are stored in tanks within the factory. Over the years the Kyle family has remained committed to investing in the industry's future, replacing their machinery as new processes and modern technology were developed.

Bulk storage facilities were installed and new equipment and machinery purchased, and nearby factories were acquired to allow the company room for further expansion. Today, nothing is left to chance; computers meter standard amounts of oils into compounding tanks, where other ingredients such as emulsifiers, salt, flavourings and colour are added.

Forward planning lies near the heart of Cardowan's success; the price of edible oils fluctuates erratically - one memorable year saw the price of palm oil double within a 12-month period, topping £1,000 a tonne - so the buying of oils from refineries at the keenest prices, sometimes months in advance, is of prime importance. Raw materials used in producing the different blends of margarine are imported from all over the world. Each oil is then refined to neutralise its distinctive taste, smell and colour before being delivered by tanker to the factory in Glasgow. The purified oil undergoes rigorous laboratory testing before being transferred to bulk storage tanks.

The Kyle family, now in its third generation with Walter Kyle's great-nephew John at the helm as managing director, have kept Cardowan Creameries as an independent family business, and are justi-fiably proud of their determination to stay at the forefront of innovation and new developments.

Above: *Van drivers outside the company's premises.*

Completely new methods have been introduced when research has shown that the new techniques are beneficial to the end product. On the other hand, however, painstaking research has in the case of some blends actually meant a return to traditional methods of production. While other manufacturers were scrapping the old established ways of working Cardowan has reinvested in traditional equipment to carry out certain processes, proving that in certain circumstances 'the old ways are the best'. Whatever the method employed, each process is governed by rigorous standards of quality control and hygiene, accredited to the ISO 9002 standards.

The soft textures of cake margarines and shortening tend to respond well to modern methods. The blends of oils are firstly chilled and worked, then fitted into individual coded packs, where natural crystallisation takes place. It was found that puff pastry margarine, however, turned out better if it was produced by

Above, both pictures: *The 1956 fire ripped through the building. The Glasgow Fire Service battled with the blaze, but could not save the factory from serious damage.*

traditional methods. The blends are cooled and solidified over ammonia chilled drums, which produces a crystal structure which the company's research and development department found to be superior to that produced by the more innovative methods. After resting for six hours, the pastry margarine is then packed by extruding on to a polythene wrapper and then into coded packs. Each margarine can contain up to four individual oils, and it is the composition of the blend that makes the all-important difference between the

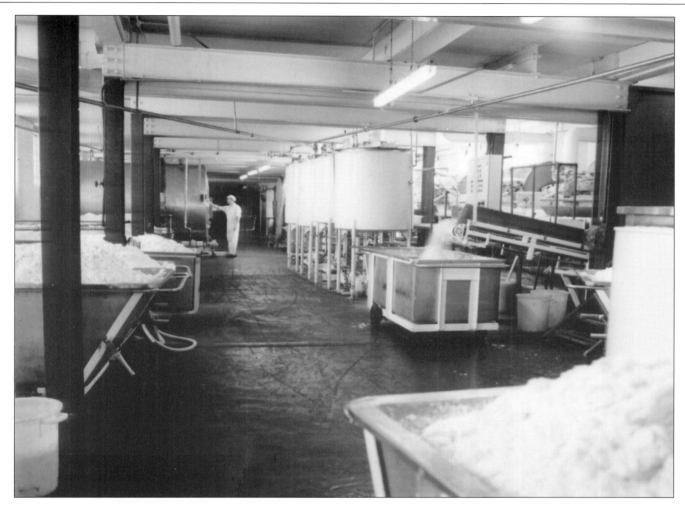

products. The margarines are continually evaluated in-house in the company's test bakery, where cakes and pastries of all kinds are produced to allow the skilled staff to evaluate the versatility and quality of the margarine. Cardowan Creameries supplies to the baking, catering and food processing industries across the board, from the small independent baker to the major food manufacturers. Their range of 45 different products reflects the differing requirements of the customer, whether it is pastry margarine, pie shortening, cake margarine - or one especially formulated for frying doughnuts.

Packed in 12.5 kilo boxes displaying such creative brand names as Waverley, Zephyr, Gamma and King Cole (a whimsical play on the name Kyle), the margarine is despatched to destinations across Britain and Ireland - and the company is today looking towards the European market.

Customer care is high on the agenda, and as well as the standard range of products blended to cover all purposes Cardowan, as a small company, are able to offer their clients a bespoke service to their own individual requirements. In addition,

on-site advice is available in the customer service department to help clients with any problems they might come up against. According to John Kyle, this kind of service is a key ingredient in the family firm's success, and their individual blend of quality, service, price and reinvestment will enable them to continue to supply customers with the traditional Scottish value that they deserve.

Above: Modern creamery methods.
Below: The premises today.

In defence of the realm

At the time of writing (1999) the Royal Ordnance Factory at Bishopton is owned by BAe but continues to fulfil its original function. Although today it is staffed by less than 300 employees, in the 1940s more than 20,000 people worked there. There can be few local people who do not know something of the work that was carried out there, as even those who never worked there themselves will know people - friends, family, former colleagues - who did. We hope therefore that this article will be of interest to everyone, although it has been written specifically with ex-employees of Bishopton in mind, to remind them of the work that went on there during wartime, 'in defence of the realm'.

To many people these brave words automatically bring to mind the uniformed armed services with which most families were closely connected during the war. Armament factories may have lacked some of the impact of the traditions and customs associated with noble naval actions, amazing regimental nicknames such as the Pig and Whistle Lads and the lonely courage of aerial combat on a wing and a prayer, but were nevertheless essential elements of the nation's defence capabilities.

The Royal Ordnance Factory at Bishopton was one of a number upon which the Forces depended for their expensive hardware, such as tanks and other weaponry, and their rapidly-used consumables such as ammunition and explosives. The latter could be as dangerous to produce as when delivered to the ultimate end user - the King's enemies. The Quality Assurance

Departments ensured that nothing but the best ever left the factory.

ROF Bishopton was built in the late 1930s and, like all ROFs, was equipped with its own development and experimental departments. Bishopton specialised in the manufacture of traditional propellants for artillery shells of all types and sizes.

Both visitors and staff were checked at the gate, as at a coal mine, to ensure that no inflammable substances (known as Contraband) were taken into the work place. All staff signed the Official Secrets Act common to employment in Government departments. Constant adherence to safety and security practices rapidly became a way of life, however strange it may have

Above: *A booklet issued to all war department staff just prior to World War II.*
Below: *The entrance to the Bishopton factory in the 1940s.*

appeared to less restricted outsiders.

For all that the machinery used in the manufacturing processes might at first glance have looked similar to that found in breweries, bakeries and dairies, the highly-skilled employees of ROF Bishopton were constantly working with volatile materials. The explosive force of these was beyond the wildest dreams of medieval alchemist and schoolboy fireworks adapters alike. Wood cellulose, foodstuff of the stag beetle's larvae, may have looked innocent enough; but when converted into paper it formed the raw material for making nitrocellulose rocket propellants. Artillery shell propellants were produced from a similar fibre, gun cotton, made from cotton linters which arrived at ROF in hard-packed bales which had to be fluffed apart before being processed.

The dried cotton was put into earthenware pans and a mixture of nitric and sulphuric acids was added. The end products, arrived at after much soaking and boiling, beating, stirring, blending and drying, were propellants varying in nitrocellulose content, designed to punch small-arms bullets and gun shells from cartridges into flight. The higher the nitrocellulose content, the greater the energy; and the greater the energy, the heavier the payload - and the further the distance travelled.

At Bishopton the manufacture of nitroglycerine - a liquid explosive of legendary power - was conducted under the most rigorous conditions, with all blending and movement being handled by remote control. The operators were well-protected from the risks inherent in processing highly corrosive substances. Some of the materials, when mixed with other normally safe chemicals, developed the property of potential self-conflagration. Carefully calculated and regulated quan-

tities of nitroglycerine emulsion and nitrocellulose were mixed in a tank containing gently stirred water. The mixture then had the water removed as the chemicals were sieved through cloth to produce a paste which

Above: The December 1939 monthly magazine issued by the factory. **Top:** A photograph taken by the Luftwaffe in 1941. Known by locals as 'early German tourists', the Luftwaffe took a number of high quality aerial photographs of potential targets. Inexplicably, Bishopton escaped attack, although nearby the nearby Clydebank shipyards were blitzed.

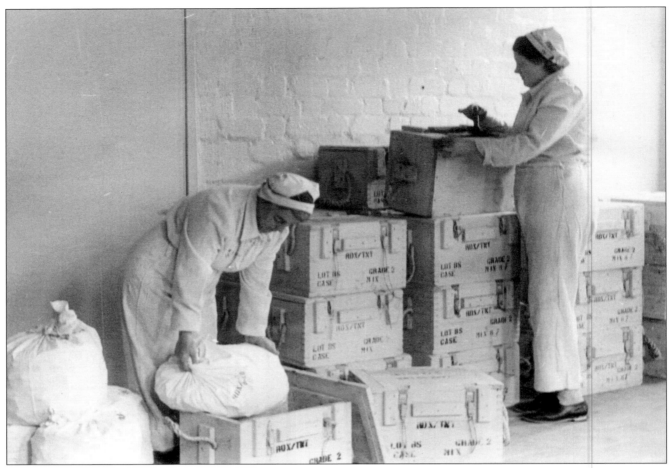

was squeezed into sheets, then cut and dried in a
current of warm air. It might have sounded harm-
less enough, but there was always the risk that
careless handling might set it off.

Old-fashioned black powder, or gunpowder, was
made with sulphur, potassium nitrate and char-
coal - a mixture which, when ignited, belched
out of the barrels of muskets and guns with a
spectacular flame up to a yard long. The char-
coal, made from coked wood, left coal-like
deposits inside weapons which had to be washed
out with hot water to make the guns safe to
refire. Smokeless propellants proved much
more efficient, producing on combustion cool,
clean gases which minimise smoke and extend
barrel life. A further benefit in camouflaged
warfare is that, with neither smoke nor flame
escaping from the barrel, there is nothing to
reveal the gun's position.

The manufacture of picrite was reminiscent of lessons
spent in school laboratories, heating and mixing, dilut-
ing and crystallising wonderfully-named chemicals
such as dicyandiamides and ammonium nitrate, the
latter well-known to farmers as a fertiliser. That thick
and unpleasant chemical, concentrated sulphuric acid,
was added, and the ensuing reaction resulted in the
formation picrite. When diluted with water the mixture
separated into picrite crystals and a dilute acid slurry.
Further cooling, filtering, drying and repeated processing produced a substance ready for the Gun Propellant

Top: The packing house. ***Above right:*** *Dancing at the
factory's Social Club - 1940s style.*

Section. All that remained to be taken care of was the
safe disposal of the dilute acid.

The dried nitroglycerine paste was transported by the
Bishopton Light Railway, which connected all departments, to the Gun Propellant Section. There it was
mixed into a stiff dough with the solvent acetone, a
liquid used by ladies to remove nail varnish. The other
ingredients - picrite, carbamite (a stabiliser to enhance
keeping qualities), and sodium cryolite (another flash
suppressor) - were added at this stage. The dough was
then cut into spaghetti-like strands which were sometimes chopped into granules for easier handling before
further drying and blending. The latter process was
vital to obtain the even quality which alone gave accu-
racy and regularity when guns were fired, qualities

which had often been lacking in earlier propellants. Rocket propellants were even more complex than gun explosives as other secret ingredients were added at the liquid mixing stages. Varying proportions of these additives were used, on a similar principle to the refinement of crude oil into different grades as fuel for oil lamps and heaters, as diesel fuel, or as different octanes of petrol for saloon and racing cars, not to mention the high octane spirits for aircraft. Manufacturing was conducted in similar conditions and by processes allied to the other Bishopton products.

Filling factories used cloth, plastic, steel, brass or alloy containers for its end products, some of which would be familiar to every teenage cadet who has fired small arms. Bishopton produced combustible cartridge cases on the other hand, paid for themselves by reducing the wear caused by inflammable cases.

The colour coding and stencilling of shell type labelling was as vital to men on active service as any instruction for use found on food and medicine packages in the home.

One of the less well-known of the vital support departments was the in-house laundry which cleaned both the specialist and the commonplace protective clothing worn by staff in engineering and design areas, laboratories and blending sections at all times.

Since the factory was built it has seen many changes. It has undertaken work to demilitarise old ammunition after the 1940-1945 war, and an Environmental Test Facility has been installed to test newly-designed weapon systems before they can safely be allowed to enter Service use.

Today, in 1999, the factory continues to produce a diverse range of propellant products for weapon systems such as the Challenger Tank, anti-air missiles and the Martin Baker Ejector Seat, a device which allows a pilot to escape safely from a fighter aircraft. However, the future of the site as a propellant producer is likely to cease in 2001 as the requirement for propellant products diminishes, and overseas companies are encouraged to bid for UK ammunition orders.

Although only a small part of the site is still in use, the whole area will need to be decontaminated to remove traces of its former activity before it can be re-developed. In the meantime wildlife is flourishing in the 2000 acres, and deer, foxes and badgers enjoy an environment which is relatively free from human interference.

Left: *Manufacture of nitrocellulose in the 1940s.*
Below: *Rail transportation of vital raw ingredients.*

Thomas Annan - Glasgow's photographic pioneer

In the early 1850s Thomas Annan moved to Glasgow from his home village of Dairsie near Cuper in Fife, to take up a position as an apprentice engraver. One of seven children, Thomas was considered artistic by those who knew him, and he soon became enthusiastic about the new and exciting phenomenon of the day - photography. Together with a friend, a trainee doctor by the name of Berwick, Thomas set up a photography business in 1855. The partnership did not last long, Berwick leaving to pursue his medical career, leaving Thomas Annan to develop the business.

From 1857 the firm operated from the bustling Sauchiehall Street, gaining patronage from the owners of the country houses and mansions around the city, keen to see their property, paintings and family recorded for posterity by the miracle of photography. Many commissions were undertaken for the owners of large properties to have their estates photographed and the prints bound in lavish volumes. Inevitably success led to expansion, and a works was established in Hamilton as early as 1859.

Right: *Charles Rennie Mackintosh, who became a friend of James Craig Annan.*
Below: *Queen Victoria's visit to Loch Katrine.*

At around this time Thomas lived next door to the sisters of David Livingstone, the famous explorer. As a result of their acquaintance Thomas was able to take what is considered to be the definitive photographic portrait of Livingstone.

Annan's reputation was such that when Queen Victoria visited Loch Katrine, Scotland to open the new water improvement scheme he was chosen to record the event photographically. Another milestone was passed in 1868 when the City of Glasgow Improvement Trust engaged Thomas Annan to make a photographic record of the slum areas before they were demolished. This is one of the first examples of the use of photography as documentary evidence.

Inevitably Thomas's sons, James and John, followed him into the business when they became old enough. James struck up a friendship with the renowned Charles Rennie Mackintosh and took the definitive photograph of him with his distinctive 'floppy bow tie' as well as dozens of contemporary images of his work. The firm were appointed official photographers for the Glasgow Exhibitions of 1888, 1901 and 1911. In 1889 the Royal Warrant was awarded to Thomas Annan and Sons by Queen Victoria. By the turn of the century the Gallery side of the business began to flourish. It became a great social occasion to view a painting by a respected artist in a dimly-lit room, and then to purchase a photo-gravure print of it. Later, it was decided to sell paintings and etchings rather than just prints. Many famous artists held shows in Annan's over the years, but one of the

most notable must have been that for L.S Lowry in 1946. All this artistic activity did not mean that photography was neglected by the company. The firm continued to take photographs of Glasgow depicting everything from street scenes and bridges to buildings and tramcars. This collection has found a variety of uses over the years and is still in demand from people undertaking research, or simply seeking an attractive framed image for their home or office.

In more recent times the company was headed by John C. Annan, under whose leadership it moved more into the Art Dealing arena, holding memorable one-man shows and supporting talented, mainly Scottish artists such as Helen M. Turner, James Watt, Hamish MacDonald, Joe Kearney, J.D Henderson, Robert Egginton, Don McNeil, Jean Bell and many others. Sadly, John C. Annan passed away in 1996, but the firm continues to be run as a family concern by his son Douglas Annan, the fifth generation to be involved with the company. The present-day Gallery at 164 Woodlands Road is only 50 yards away from where the story began. An impressive selection of original paintings can be found at the Gallery, along with the collection of old photographs and a comprehensive restoration and picture framing service. The company has come a long way since it was established almost a century and a half ago, but the philosophy of providing customers with a friendly and efficient service has remained the same. Thomas Annan would have been proud of that.

Above: *The premises today.*

A taste of success

A farm in the warm countryside of southern Italy is a very long way from Queen Mary Street, Glasgow - and it would have seemed even further in 1895, when transport was far slower and decidedly more limited than today. It was with a true pioneering spirit, therefore, that Serafino Crolla exchanged the sunshine of Picinisco for the less predictable climes of Scotland. With him was his six year old son Giuseppe, whose mother had died in childbirth.

Traditional Italian ice cream was the business Serafino decided to set up in, and with little Giuseppe helping wherever he could the shop in Queen Mary Street was soon up and running. Realising that ice cream tended to be a seasonal product that, particularly in the British Isles, had a natural slack period in winter time, Serafino shrewdly placed hot peas on his menu to complement his ices, soft drinks and sodas.

It was a difficult time, however, for the young Italian, who found that bringing up a child alone while trying to succeed in business was more challenging than he had imagined.

Above right: One of the first motorised vans.
Below: The original shop in Main Street, Bridgeton.

After five years at the shop he rented the premises to friends and returned to Italy. The young Giuseppe Crolla could not forget the few years he had spent growing up in Glasgow, however, and in 1913 he returned to Scotland, bringing with him his wife Serafina. He opened a second shop in Clydebank at 67 Glasgow Road.

Even then the clouds of war were looming overhead and the following year saw the outbreak of World War I. In 1917 Giuseppe Crolla returned to Italy with Serafina and his young family of three children, leaving his shops under management. When the war ended in 1918 he

The years of the second world war were difficult ones for an Italian family living in Britain; Giuseppe was interned in Australia and his three sons, Domenico, Lorenzo and Sabatino, were interned in Canada. Serafina was left to run the business alone with her two sons, Dario and Alcide, and daughter, Ida.

After the war things began to get back on track; the distinctive flavour of Crolla ice cream proved to be very popular, and the product was soon much in demand. By 1950 the Crolla family had started up an ice cream factory, and had 30 vans selling their delicious ice cream around the streets of Glasgow.

Today the firm still supplies ice cream vans, but also supplies to shops, cafés, wholesalers, restaurants and hotels. Naturally enough, it has its competitors too in other small ice cream manufacturers around the area. The company has found that having a firm favourite to offer is a distinct advantage, and Crolla's traditional old fashioned café flavour has established itself as a leader in the popularity stakes.

And what of the future? The family is not satisfied to simply sit back and rest on their earlier successes. Continued expansion forms part of their plans for the coming years, and their eyes are firmly fixed on pastures new....south of the border. Look out, England!

Peter Crolla, Serafino's great-grandson, has today established the fourth generation of Crollas - a family firm in the true sense of the word. Together with their customers and loyal staff they look forward to the next stage in the history of the Crolla Ice Cream Company.

Above left: *One of today's delivery lorries.*
Top: *A 1950s scene with a Crolla ice-cream van in the centre.*

tried desperately to return to his business but was unable to do so until 1920. When at last he got back to Glasgow he was horrified to find that the managers he had left in charge had taken over control of both shops. Giuseppe was left with nothing.

Failure was not a word in Giuseppe Crolla's book, however, and he started once again from scratch, building up his next ice-cream business at the Premier Café in Main Street, Bridgeton. He made the basement below the shop into his workshop, and it was here, with the aid of ice and salt, that he produced his ice cream. Milk, sugar and cornflour were the main ingredients back then - a basic recipe that has changed over the years. A typical ice cream today would contain milk, sugar, butter and as well as other ingredients like stabilisers and emulsifiers.

In spite of the shortage of funds and the difficulties of expansion, the fledgling business gradually began to prosper. Eventually the Crollas were able to acquire both the adjoining properties, the fish and chip shop that lay on one side and the newsagents on the other.

Glasgow's best-bread family

Local families have been enjoying McGhee's range of morning rolls, pies and cakes for more than sixty-five years. In that time, successive generations of the McGhee family have supervised the firm's move to new premises, invested in state-of-the-art machinery and put into place a variety of new managerial, administrative and supervisory practices to increase efficiency and comply with the new and stringent regulations governing food production. But, significant as they have been for the company and its workforce, these changes have not affected McGhee's customers who have been able to depend on the firm for both daily needs and speciality cakes since 1934, when Dugald McGhee first began baking in Maryhill.

Thirty-four year old Dugald, a former bakery van salesman, chose the Maryhill district as his location because of its central location and because of its thriving business climate, which assured a ready market for bread and cakes amongst the workforces of Maryhill's major commercial and industrial companies. Dugald and his wife ran one shop and two wholesale vans, and baked a full range of bakery products. McGhee's goods soon became popular locally, and within three years the firm had moved from Springbank Street, Queen's Cross, to a bakehouse in Oran Street, which was to be its home for the next 22 years.

McGhee's was well-established by the time the war arrived, so in spite of the fat and sugar shortages, which meant cutting back on cake production, the firm was able to survive.

Above left: *Dugald McGhee (1900 - 1957), founder of the company.*
Below: *From left to right: Douglas McGhee, James McGhee (sons of the founder), Dugald McGhee (the founder) and Calder McGhee (son of the founder).*

After the war the business began to expand, and on 30th December 1950 it became a limited company, D McGhee and Sons Limited, with the founder and his four sons holding one share apiece. Dugald McGhee sadly died in 1957, leaving the company in the hands of sons Calder, Jim, Douglas and Gavin.

The business continued to prosper, and in the late 1960s plans were made to move again, this time to an impressive, purpose-built bakery complex, to be constructed on a cleared three-and-a-half acre site at 19 Murano Street. Sadly Douglas died just before moving to the new premises. These premises, comprising bakery, garage, workshop and offices, were opened in 1969, and the extensive brick building with towering twin flour silos and its 60' aluminium chimney soon became a local landmark, while the staff were immediately struck by how much better the working conditions were, The bakehouse itself was fitted out with the most up-to-date equipment available, such as the two machines to wash utensils which cut down on labour and increased hygiene standards, while the doors in the despatch area were controlled by an electronic eye which operated the doors automatically, ensuring that exhaust fumes from the vehicles never came into contact with the products. An impressive suite of offices provided comfortable and well-equipped accommodation for the office staff, while staff and workers also benefited from locker rooms with shower baths, and a modern canteen with excellent amenities. The site also provided full plant maintenance facilities, where repairs to any of the bakehouse's intricate machines could be carried out, and a mechanics' section for service and repairs to the fleet of delivery vans. There was also a spacious storeroom and an incinerator for disposing of waste, making the site virtually self-contained.

The high investment in new buildings and technology soon paid off; productivity was increased, allowing penetration into a wider geographical marketplace and moving more towards the major high street retailers as the traditional corner shop, which had always been one of the company's principal markets, became an increasingly rare sight. The move to Murano Street has brought other advantages, too; as the company owns the site, there is always potential for further development, and indeed two additional wings have already been added to the original structure. The introduction of new standards and approved working practices across the industry means that procedures and facilities are constantly under review; hygiene and quality control systems have been implemented by a specialist management team, while processing plant, offices, information/communication technology and staff facilities have all been included in the company's upgrading programme designed to maintain its prominent position in a fiercely competitive market place.

The business is now in the hands of the third generation. Current managing director is Gordon, Calder's son, with Gavin's son, Stuart, as sales director and Calder's other son, Ian as production director. Gavin has sadly passed away, but in 1996, Calder, aged 70, and nominally retired from the company, had the honour of being appointed president of the Scottish Association of Master Bakers. This is a fitting tribute to the expertise and skill of the second generation of McGhees - an expertise and skill which is very much in evidence in the third generation as well, as thousands of daily customers who enjoy goods baked by this family firm will testify.

Above: *Calder, James and Gavin planning further developments at the new bakery.*

Pioneering excellence in education

Generations of Glasgow-trained teachers may well remember the plaque in the Dundas Vale Teachers' Centre which bore the legend, 'Train up a child in the way he should go and when he is old he will not depart from it.' This principle was central to the beliefs of David Stow, a Victorian philanthropist and one of the greatest innovators and pioneers in the history of Scottish education, after whom Stow College is named.

David Stow was born in Paisley on 17 May 1793 into a family with strong Christian beliefs. He was educated at Paisley Grammar School, studying English and Classics, before embarking on a career in commerce. Glasgow attracted him, and he moved there in 1811. Poverty, overcrowding, squalor and disease predominated in Glasgow at that time, and the only way for the poor to gain an education was through Sabbath Schools, where the rudiments of the Christian faith and of reading and writing were taught. David was a member of the Tron Church in Gallowgate; he taught at Sabbath Schools and tried hard to persuade parents to send their children along. However, even his tireless canvassing for pupils brought less than a third of the children in the Tron Parish to the school, and in other parishes where Sabbath Schools were run with less enthusiasm attendance was even lower. Determined that there should be a more effective way of teaching the young before they were led astray, in 1826 David Stow founded an Infant School for boys and girls under six.

Stow's teaching methods were revolutionary; his 'picturing out' lessons, using visual aids, were an entirely new concept, and there was a playground, which was quite unheard; discipline was firm but kindly, and Stow combined his progressive methods with a firm Christian approach to life. The new school aroused a great deal of interest, and a Juvenile Department was begun in Saltmarket in 1831. Sadly, David's wife Marion died of a malignant fever in the same year, and it was several years before David recovered from this tragic loss. However, in 1836 he went on to found the Normal Training Seminary at Dundas Vale in Cowcaddens; born out of David Stow's belief that properly trained teachers of all denominations were the key to good educational practice, this was the first purpose-built teacher training college in Great Britain.

Above: *David Stow, a Victorian philanthropist, after whom Stow College is named.*
Below: *How the College would have appeared when it opened in 1934.*

During the years which followed, Stow continued to fight for the principles he believed in, and in spite of opposition from the Established Church he succeeded in keeping teacher training in Glasgow open to students of any denomination. He died in 1864, eight years prior to the passing of the Education Act which made education both free and compulsory for Scottish children under the age of ten.

A remarkable man who made education history and had a great influence on the theory and practice of teacher training and classroom learning, David Stow has been a continual source of inspiration to those who have followed, and when in 1934 Glasgow's ground-breaking 'Trades School' first opened its doors to apprentices and journeymen of all types, the name chosen for this new institution was Stow College.

Opened on the day the Queen Mary was launched on the Clyde, Stow College was Glasgow's first purpose-built further education college and only the second such college of its kind in Scotland, and its aim was to help the workers and companies of Clydeside towards economic recovery by teaching them more about their trades and enabling them to keep up with the latest technologies and theories.

During the second world war it became a training college for Forces staff, and Rolls Royce took over much of the building for aero engine manufacture; after the war, with the Government committed to the expansion of further education, Stow College had a vital role to play, and its staff were instrumental in the establishment of other centres of learning in the city including the Glasgow College of Nautical Studies and the Glasgow College of Technology, now Glasgow Caledonian University.

In recent years Stow College has adapted to the city's changing economy, offering training in management, computing and electronics and other skills relevant to today's world of high technology. At the forefront of innovation in learning and acknowledged as Glasgow's Centre of Excellence, with links with Glasgow Caledonian University and the University of Paisley, Stow College offers the ideal learning environment for the student of today. Just as David Stow had sought to meet the educational needs of his time, so Stow College has remained true to that ideal and will continue to do so, helping Glasgow meet whatever economic and industrial challenges may lie ahead, and perpetuating the progressive thinking and the sound values of David Stow.

Top: *The College in the 1960s.* ***Above left:*** *A visit to the College by the Rev Alexander McDonald.*

A Taste of Fleet Success

O n 20th November, 1950, a new business venture was launched in Newton Mearns: a general coach hire company was established under the now-familiar name of Southern Coaches. Two of the three founder directors were local men - William McIntyre and William Jamieson both lived in Newton Mearns, where, prior to founding Southern Coaches, the former had been a motor contractor and the latter a chemist. Robert Wallace, the third founder director, was a farmer from Stewarton, in Ayrshire.

The company commenced operations with just one vehicle which was by no means new, but business clearly got off to a good start, because at a meeting of the directors, chaired by Mr McIntyre and held in the Registered Office at 139 St Vincent Street, Glasgow on 16th March 1951, some four months after the venture began, it was unanimously decided that a second bus should be acquired. This was to be a much newer Leyland Tiger, to be purchased at a cost of £3640. Minutes of the meeting record that the transaction was to be financed by a bank loan from the Union Bank of Scotland in the amount of £2750, and the remaining sum was to be covered by loans from two of the directors, Mr Wallace and Mr Jamieson, who each

agreed to lend £500 to the company, repayable at a rate of interest of six per cent a year. It is not recorded how long the Company was expected to take to repay its Directors; however, their confidence was fully justified and history has proved that the investment was a wise one.

Within a couple of years the fleet had expanded a hundredfold and more; records for 1953 indicate that two Bedford coaches were acquired during that year, and Maudslay, Tilling Stevens and AEC Regal vehicles are also listed. As operations expanded, larger premises were called for, and the company relocated from Newton Mearns to Lochlibo Road, Barrhead, from where it still operates. Meanwhile the fleet continued to grow, with more Bedfords, an Albion Victor and a Commer Avenger being purchased before the end of the decade.

Above: The company's first vehicle - a Leyland Tiger.
Above left: Mr Robert Wallace, who died in 1992 at the age of 76.
Below: A Bedford Coach once owned by Southern

The company's reliable and affordable service proved popular with the local community, and it soon became a well-established concern. In the mid-1960 two of the founder directors, William McIntyre and William Jamieson, decided to resign from the company and go back to their original professions, leaving Robert Wallace to run the now-flourishing company. Robert was joined by his wife Mary, who became company secretary.

As a family-run concern, the company continued to invest in its fleet, running a number of Ford and Bedford vehicles with Plaxton and Duple bodies, one Ford with a Burlingham body, and a Commer Avenger Mk III. Southern Coaches were a familiar sight on Glasgow's roads, and it was around this time that the company began to assign fleet names to individual coaches, painted on the rear as part of the livery; people may remember travelling on the Southern Pride, the Southern Queen, the Southern Monarch or the Southern Knight.

Southern Coaches' fleet carried on growing until at one point some 30 vehicles were in operation. Fewer vehicles are owned by the company today. The directors are constantly alert to the changing requirements of their customers, and current policy is to operate a smaller fleet, but to concentrate on investing in new, top-of-range vehicles for executive-style travel. In line with this policy, the present Southern Coaches fleet consists of two 18-seater mini-coaches and 16 large coaches with seating for up to 57 passengers. The newest vehicle is an immaculate 51-seater Volvo Vanhool with a Belgium-made body, providing the ultimate in comfort and luxury.

The company continues its policy of concentrating on local work as much as possible, running a holiday service to Blackpool and operating a variety of luxury tours which cater for all tastes - from ski trips to golf tours, from school trips to senior

citizens outings, and from distillery visits to business meetings and conference transportation. Other services include airport transfers, cruise liner shore excursions and city tours, and coaches are always available for private hire.

Sons Robert (Junior) and David Wallace have joined their parents as directors of the company, and since the death of Robert (Senior) in 1992 Southern Coaches has been run by the three remaining directors. It is very much a family business, experienced in meeting the needs and expectations both of the local community and of visitors to the region, and family and staff are proud that so many people, not only Glaswegians but tourists from further afield, have happy memories of holidays and excursions courtesy of Southern Coaches. Now approaching its 50th anniversary, the company is looking forward to a new Millennium in which it will continue to provide the fast, friendly and reliable service upon which its reputation has been built.

Above: *Another Bedford coach.*
Below: *One of the company's fleet today.*

Springburn Park in the 1950s as hundreds gathered by the bandstand to watch the Temperance King and Queen lead the way across the lawns.

Acknowledgments

Margaret Forrest at the Health Education Board for Scotland, The Womens Royal Voluntary Service; Douglas Annan at The Annan Gallery; William Doig ARPS, EFIAP; Nick Baldwin, transport writer, Somerset; Meegan Taylor-Smith at Strathclyde Fire Brigade Headquarters; Jeff Holmes at the SNS Group; Mr Joe Smith and the Glasgow Fire Service; J. Ramsay Fecit; Enda Ryan and the staff at the local studies section of the Mitchell Library

Thanks are also due to Andrew Mitchell who penned the editorial text, Margaret Wakefield and Mike Kirke for their copywriting skills